COLLEGE DEGREE IN 3

A GUIDE FOR COMPLETING COLLEGE IN LESS THAN FOUR YEARS

J. WILSON BOWMAN, Ph.D

COLLEGE DEGREE IN 3

A Guide For Completing College In Less Than Four Years

©2009 by J. Wilson Bowman

Inquiries, book orders, etc. should be addressed to:
R.J. Enterprises, P. O. Box 1034,
Skyland, NC 28776.

Originally Designed, Edited, and Typeset by the Holly Rudelitsch
Artwork by Biljana Bosevska Kroll
Graphics and Internal Design by Albert Epp
Cover Photo Of Tuskegee University

Library of Congress Cataloging-in-Publication Data

College Degree In 3 First Edition

ISBN 978-0-9663562-1-2
Printed in the U S A

Bowman, J. Wilson
1. Education
2. Public Schools
3. College Planning

Dedication

To those serious students
who plan to complete
a quality college education
in less than the number of years
which seems typical in the 21st century.

To Koi, Xia, Medina, India, Jasmine and Kaela
my granddaughters and grandsons
Ayomide, Branford and Christopher
whom I hope will read this book
when they start to think about college.

Acknowledgments

This book is the culmination of several years of work and the assistance of many people. Specifically, Holly Rudelitsch who did all of the original layout work on the book; Biljana, a young artist working on her degree that has since been completed; the numerous people who read and offered suggestions like E. Shaw, a college professor; J. Aziz, M.D.; M. Hines, Ed.D. retired public school Administrator and E. McAfee, Esq. But most of all to my husband, a retired California Administrator, Richard, I owe the greatest praise. His belief in the project, his amazing talent in identifying areas that needed special attention and his ability to keep me focused have been paramount. Without his efforts, this book would not have been completed. It was he who identified the literary agent who marshaled the project through completion. He is indeed the *"wind beneath my wings"*.

Foreword

"Once you make a decision, the universe conspires to make it happen."
Ralph Waldo Emerson - May 25, 1803 – April 27, 1882

The years spent in college are one of the most important periods of time in the lives of those of us who choose this path. It is a time of experimentation, learning self-sufficiency and being responsible for yourselves without someone looking over your shoulder. It is a time for maturation of your decision-making. One of the most important decisions you will ever make will be what your life's work will be.

If a student can identify his or her field of endeavor as early as the first two years of high school, then that student is ready to chart a course to finish college and get on with life, whether that be in the job market or attaining a higher degree. However, even if the student hasn't made up his or her mind about their course of study, there is still the possibility of being able to accelerate through school.

With tuition continuously rising, it is imperative that attention be focused on planning as one takes the path to and through college. The search for available scholarships and organizations which help to fund education will be much more successful when started early, i.e., while in high school. This early planning both financially and educationally will be beneficial to you, the student and your family. The average costs of college tuitions are rising yearly at rates of between 6 to 8% and the cost of a number of private colleges has risen to above $45,000 a year.

Dr. Bowman has laid out an outstanding blueprint to finishing college in less than the standard four years saving you both time and money.

This book takes you through the planning stage in high school, finding out what you have an aptitude for, taking advanced placement courses. It offers many practical points of advice from navigating the class selection process to dealing with some of the pitfalls of campus life such as drugs and peer pressure.

This book is the most helpful that I have seen on the subject of accelerating through college, so I urge you to read it and do what is necessary to obtain your college degree in less than 4 years! With the right amount of effort, you can do it!

John Aziz, MD

John Aziz, MD is an anesthesiologist. He received his Bachelors Degree from Cornell University in Biochemistry & his MD Degree from Rutgers Medical School.

About The Author

Dr. J. Wilson Bowman is a graduate of Tuskegee University and the University of California at Berkeley. She is an educator in the true sense of the word. Graduating as chemistry major, she moved through the ranks from secondary teacher to college administrator. She has served as a consultant to the Alameda County Public School system in Alameda, California; the California Commission for Teacher Preparation and Licensing in Sacramento, California and the California State Department of Education. Additionally, she served as an evaluator for the U.S. Office of Education and as a consultant for the American Council on Education in Washington, D. C. Dr Bowman has taught at a number of California Colleges including Merritt College in Oakland, Golden Gate College, in San Francisco, J. F. Kennedy University, in Orinda, and San Jose State College. For more than eight years she served as associate vice president for academic affairs at Diablo Valley College, leaving there to become, vice president of Academic Affairs at Compton College in southern California.

In 1998 she moved to Asheville, with her husband Richard a native Ashevillian, where she served as director of the YWCA before becoming a member of the faculty at Mars Hill College. In 2006 she joined the Education staff at the University of North Carolina at Asheville. Dr. Bowman is indeed a seasoned educator who has had the opportunity to participate in the management, accreditation and evaluation of numerous college programs. She is uniquely qualified to address the topics in the book, "College Degree in Three".

A Note from the Author

Let me tell you about Jared, a student I met before writing this book. When I met Jared he was in his 4th year of college – but according to his calculations he had about two more years before graduation. I wondered why. He was a good student, having graduated from high school early with a 3.8 GPA.

Jared completed all of the senior high school requirements early and was allowed to work full time to start saving for college. With such a good start, why was he so far behind? From my conversation with him, I discovered that he was given no college advisement, attended no college planning sessions and was given no information about scholarships. Neither was he told about dual enrollment (a way of taking college credit courses while in high school). Jared had been a quiet student focused on making good grades so that he could go to college. He didn't talk to anyone about his plans and no one bothered to talk to him. Since he was the first in his family to attend college, there was no one at home to guide him or assist him in making the leap from high school to college. He admitted that he had no idea what he would select as a "major" even though he had been accepted.

The first semester in college he was a loner. He did not know how to find study groups; he did not know that many professors place previous tests given year after year on file in the library. Basically, he did not understand the "college culture". His first year on campus, he took a full load (12 units) and did so each semester because somewhere he had read that a full load was important to obtain scholarship assistance. Though he had completed two full semesters, they were without focus. By the time he had completed two years, he realized that "learning-how-to-college" had been costly. Deciding late on a major, he realized that with his chosen major it was like starting over, and it was going to take him at least five additional semesters to finish.

This book is too late for Jared, but hopefully it will be of value to other students and parents in understanding the college maze.

Introduction

A report published by Education Trust found that only 37% of first time freshman entering four-year bachelor degree programs actually complete their degree within four-years; another 26% take 5 or 6 years. The remaining 37% either do not get their degree at all, or complete their course work in more than six years. It is information like this that is the impetus for this publication.

The question that will be addressed in this book is whether or not it is possible to complete college in less than four years? The most immediate answer is—of course you can if you attend summer school each year. This book is designed to give a heads-up on the kind of information one needs to know in order to complete college in less than four-years, without spending each summer in school.

Even before high school is over, there are decisions to be made that will affect the rest of your life. One of those is whether or not to attend college. A decade ago a college degree could be considered a luxury. The world has experienced a tremendous change since the 20th century when many people could have a successful career with only a high school degree. One could start at an entry-level job and work up to management. Many of these were manufacturing jobs that did not require a college education, today those blue-collar jobs have moved overseas. According to the Bureau of Labor Statistics the job market of this decade will require workers who have more technical and professional skills, the kind that require college training.

This publication is focused on two kinds of students, those who identified early in high school that college was a serious choice and those who are finishing high school and have just realized the importance of a college degree and think 'man, I'd better get into school, someplace! It is primarily for students who have made the decision to cut the umbilical cord, attend a four-year college, and graduate in less than four-years. It will facilitate the successful movement of the student through the college maze. It assumes that the student has been admitted to or has decided to attend college, and provides information vital to understanding how colleges are structured and the steps involved in getting a college degree in a timely manner.

Graduating seniors have a host of challenges as they contemplate one of the most serious decisions of their young life. They will need to evaluate the choices made in high school, comparing these to the requirements for admission to college. They will need to evaluate their prior academic record and their ability to commit to the rigorous program of academics that characterize college.

Smart choices in high school are a major requirement in completing college in less than four-years. If these choices have not been made it will be a bit more difficult, but not impossible, to meet the established goal without at least one summer session.

For some, there was never a question about attending college, and for others it is a decision yet to be made. Each year thousands of students and their parents or guardians are faced with the decisions regarding college attendance. To go, or not to go? To stay close to home, or not? Two-year community college or a four-year college? Public or private college? Or perhaps waiting a year before entering college? Whatever the circumstances, deciding to get a college degree is one of the most important decisions you will make. As there are thousands of young people making these decisions, there are thousands of colleges opening their doors, eagerly awaiting the new crop of students. Rather than wait for students to inquire, today colleges are pursuing prospects with direct mail, especially students who are doing well in high school and have completed the SAT I, SAT II (Scholastic Assessment Test) and/or ACT (American College Test) successfully.

For every student who wants to go to college, there is a perfect college for them. There is a definite difference between those who want to go college and those who want to get a college degree. People go to college for a variety of reasons. Some go hoping to be recognized by a recruiting scout, some go with the primary reason of finding a mate, some go simply wanting to get away from home, others go because their parents expect them to, and then there are those who are career oriented .

For those who fall into the latter group, and want to get an education in the least expensive and shortest amount of time, a basic plan is vital:

1. Define your goal, i.e. to obtain a degree in_____
2. Determine the steps necessary to accomplish the goal
3. Determine the factors that may inhibit achieving the goal
4. Develop strategies to increase positive outcomes
5. Design an educational plan
6. Develop a chronological time line of action
7. Monitor your progress. This book will assist you in accomplishing these basic steps.

While this book addresses serious students who want to get a good college education from an accredited institution that is affordable, in the least amount of time, every student can benefit from reading this book. If you can manage to follow just some of the advice, you'll be more likely to finish in four-years or less.

What Is Special About This Book?

The major feature of this book is the focus on pre-college-preparation of students in high school. Emphasis on decision making is the thread that links all of the topics. Two major perspectives, completing college in less than four years and the importance of prior planning have been used as a guiding force in putting this book together. In a broader sense, I believe that anyone interested or engaged in the instruction or supervision of teenagers will find some information of value in this publication.

Unique in this book is the range of ideas covered in a relatively fast paced format. Topic headings are designed to help readers understand the layout and use of this book. Realistic scenarios specifically on aspects of the college experience are referenced throughout.

This book is divided into five sections, the first section is intended to share information that is vital for students in high school to consider if they plan to complete high school prepared to enter college. If students understand the relationship between high school experiences and the impact that choices in high school have on success in college, they can be better prepared. The second section sets forth a way of planning for the college experience, with a discussion of the role of initial placement tests and the challenges associated with adjusting to college. Specific assistance is shared to help students decide on which course of action they might follow in deciding on a major. Section three clarifies and amplifies those topics that are important in being successful at the college level. It is an effort to deliver on what the subtitle of this book promises: an action plan for completing college in less than four years. Section four presents the challenges that are relatively common for first time college students. Included in this section you will find information about time management, roommates and the non-academic hurdles that can wreck an otherwise successful start to the life of a college student.

The fifth section is seldom discussed in books that are intended to help students make the transition from high school to college. This is one of the unique characteristics of my book. This section discusses factors that can seriously interfere with completing college. Section five is a brief but significant section focused on factors that I call the "Dangerous 5", situations that exist at every college that must not be ignored as one considers becoming a college graduate.

Taken as a whole, this tiny book is intended to help the reader think through the issues that must be addressed if completing college in less than four years is a serious goal.

TABLE OF CONTENTS

5

COLLEGE DEGREE IN 3   BY WILSON J. BOWMAN

Thinking About College

COLLEGE CHOICES

Few places in the industrial world offer as many college choices as the United States. There are so many different kinds of colleges from which a student can choose that making a commitment can be difficult.

There are many different kinds of "colleges" such as:
• Community colleges • Private colleges • State colleges
• Historically Black colleges • Religious colleges • Ivy League colleges • Female only colleges • Male only colleges
• Military colleges • Tribal colleges • On-line colleges.

There are also those that focus on the professions like medicine, law and veterinary medicine, to identify a few. There are, of course, some cross-over colleges. For instance, a law college might also be a state college and an historically Black college. In *Bowman's America's Black and Tribal Colleges,* one can view a listing of the more than one hundred original Historical Black colleges, in addition to a listing of the American Indian Colleges. GM's Chevrolet divisions developed a guide to the 25 best colleges for Hispanics, which include seven colleges in California, four in Texas and three in Massachusetts. Students in the United States are fortunate to have numerous and various choices from which to select a college. Options vary from the 23+ campuses of the New York System to the tiny Alaska Pacific University in Anchorage with less than 500 students. Each of the more than 3,000 colleges that exist is focused for a specific clientele clearly expressed in their philosophical statement. Regardless of the specific college, there are basically five components to a successful college experience:

1. Finances
2. Study Skills
3. Time management
4. Relationships
5. College catalogue

It is how you assign value to these five components, and channel your energies to address these, that will determine your success in college. All of these components will impact your goal of getting out of college in less than four-years. Each of these will be discussed with emphasis on the academics and achieving your goal.

PLANNING AHEAD

In order to decrease the amount of time required to complete college it is vital that planning occurs early in high school. Identifying possible college choices, collecting resources such as copies of college catalogues, previewing list of majors and even identifying a college major should be accomplished as soon as possible. Identify college courses that can be completed before the 12th grade and preview other course options available at the local community college accessible to high school students and transferable to the four-year institution. Students who put in place a plan for making the best use of their high school years will find themselves well positioned to complete college in less than four-years. This would include making smart choices of classes to meet school requirements such as, advance placement classes and taking advantage of the op-

8

portunity to enroll at the local community college, an option often available for juniors and seniors.

Students who have maintained above average grades can request the opportunity for dual enrollment at nearby four-year institutions. Dual enrollment is an arrangement in which colleges and high schools agree to allow students in high school to take courses for which they earn both college and high school credit. These courses are separate and different from the Advanced Placement courses taught at the high school, by high school instructors.

Dual enrollment courses, may be taught at the high school, a community college or at a four college campus. These are college courses taught by college instructors. According to the Center for Educational Statistics 38 states offer dual enrollment, providing opportunity for advanced classes such as foreign language and mathematics, classes that might not be available at the high school. These courses can significantly decrease the number of classes required at the college level.

Colleges look for students who have been active participants in extra curricular and community activities. Depending upon the college major selected, these activities can be evaluated and used to meet certain college requirements. With proper planning most of the high school requirements can be completed prior to the final semester of the senior year. This would leave a full semester for dual enrollment classes that could be completed before leaving home for college.

If you have not put into place a plan that included completing some college courses before the end of the 12th grade, it is still not too late to make the effort to complete college in less than four-years. There are some basics that must be recognized. Most colleges are divided into two semesters, fall and spring.

Depending upon the major, the college degree requires a completion of 128–150 semester units. Science and music majors, because of lab classes, often require more actual class hours than listed semester hours. The 130+ units equates to 16 or more credit hours per semester for eight semesters, which equals four-years. Therefore, without serious planning and utilizing the time available in high school, you will have to take more than 16 credit hours per semester to complete college in four-years.

To get a head start on college once you have decided that you definitely plan to attend, here are some of the steps that would be helpful:

1. Contact the college for a catalogue.

2. Decide on a major.

3. Review the courses required for the major.

4. Meet with a high school counselor to see if some of the courses can be completed during the junior or senior year.

5. Design a temporary three-year schedule based on the major selected.

6. Contact the high school counselor or a financial aid counselor at a local college for the financial aid application by the first semester of your 12th grade year.

7. Sit down with your parents to review the financial aid documents.

8. Completed documents must be submitted in a timely manner.

These should be accomplished prior to completing high school and will help tremendously in preparing for a stress free college experience.

Before you select a college to attend try: the College Navigator from the National Center for Education Statistics at nces.ed.gov/collegenavigator. Here you can get a print out of the latest data on expenses, aid, enrollment, admission and graduation rates, majors amd a Google map pinpointing location. If you would like a virtual tour of the campuses try CampusTours.com. This site links to video tours of nearly 1,000 schools.

COLLEGE PLANNING CHECKLIST

9th Grade	10th Grade
☐ Make a career path decision	☐ Focus on grades
☐ Start an online scholarship search	☐ Develop possible scholarships list
☐ Complete assignments before date	☐ Complete assignments in advance
☐ Develop good study practices	☐ Get to know your instructors
☐ Get to know your teachers	☐ Develop time management skills
☐ Develop healthy living habits	☐ Maintain good study habits
☐ Ask parents about the 529 College Saving Plan*	

11th Grade	12th Grade
☐ Keep grades up	☐ Revise and update college list
☐ Share your plans with parents	☐ Use scholarship list for support
☐ Develop a list of college choices	☐ Take the SAT
☐ Continue developing the list of scholarships	☐ Enroll in Dual Enrollment Program
☐ Request college applications	☐ Complete college applications
☐ Investigate dual enrollment	☐ Complete / send financial aid papers
☐ Meet with school counselor	☐ Complete all scholarship applications
☐ Review your scholarship options list	☐ Prepare letters for scholarships
☐ Obtain financial aid papers for review	☐ Review award letters
☐ Practice completing FAFSA papers	☐ Apply for private loans
☐ Take the PSAT/ACT	☐ Discuss all of your work with parents
☐ Attend college fairs	☐ Get help in completing all documents
☐ Visit the campuses of choice	☐ Make your final choices/send in applications

11

*529 College Savings Plan is an education saving plan available in every state. The plan earnings are tax-exempt when the funds are used for educational expenses and no federal income tax is due on withdrawals. There are no limitations on who can open an account. Funds can be used at any accredited school. The 529 plans are either prepaid or saving plans. In Prepaid plans all or part of the costs of an in-state public college education is prepaid. It can be converted for use at private and out-of-state colleges. Saving plans work like a 401k or IRA by investing contributions in mutual funds or similar investments.

LEAVING HOME

Leaving home for college is a giant step. As the end of the senior year in high school approaches some serious questions regarding this giant step must be considered. Students will wonder - "am I ready to leave home?" What about my friends? Some students will enroll in a local community college so that they can stay at home. Some may feel they can't afford the four-year college away from home. Some, because they have not decided on a major, may want to wait a while to get used to the idea of being on their own. Still others are simply not ready to leave the nest. Some questions that must be answered are: How far away from home are you willing to go? How important is it that your friends will attend the college you have selected? Are you prepared to make the decisions that will be required in a timely manner? And finally, are you serious about getting a college education?

Could Kipling have been thinking about youth making a major life change when he wrote:

> *If you can keep your head when all about you*
> *Are losing theirs and blaming it on you.*
> *If you can trust yourself when all men doubt you,*
> *But make allowance for their doubting too;*
> *If you can wait and not be tired by waiting,*
> *Or being lied about, don't deal in lies,*
> *Or being hated, don't give way to hating.*
> *And yet don't look too good, nor talk too wise*
>
> *If you can dream – and not make dreams your master;*
> *If you can think – and not make thoughts your aim;*
> *If you can meet with triumph and disaster*
> *And treat those two imposters just the same;*
> *If you can bear to hear the truth you've spoken*
> *Twisted by knaves to make a trap for fools,*
> *Or watch the things you gave your life to, broken,*
> *And stoop and build 'em up with worn-out tools;*

13

If you can make one heap of all your winnings
And risk it on one turn of pitch and toss
And lose, and start again at your beginnings
And never breathe a word about your loss;
If you can force your heart and nerve and sinew
To serve your turn long after they are gone,
And so hold on when there is nothing in you
Except the Will which says to them: "Hold on!"

If you can talk with crowds and keep your virtue,
Or walk with kings – nor lose the common touch,
If neither woes nor loving friends can hurt you,
If all men count with you, but none too much;
If you can fill the unforgiving minute
With sixty seconds' worth of distance run,
Yours is the Earth and everything that's in it,
And - which is more - you'll be a Man, my son!

Rudyard Kipling 1865 - 1936

14

Then I think you can consider yourself ready to tackle the scary task of leaving home.

COURSE PLANNING WORKSHEET

Recommended College Prep Subjects								
	GRADES		GRADES		GRADES		GRADES	
	FALL	SPRING	FALL	SPRING	FALL	SPRING	FALL	SPRING
English (4 units)	——	——	——	——	——	——	——	——
U.S. History/Gov. (1 units)	——	——	——	——	——	——	——	——
Mathematics (4 units)	——	——	——	——	——	——	——	——
Science (2 units, 2 lab science units)	——	——	——	——	——	——	——	——
Foreign Language (2 units)	——	——	——	——	——	——	——	——
Electives: Arts, English, History Social Science, Visual/Performing (4 units)	——	——	——	——	——	——	——	——
Computer Science + Other Courses (4 units)	——	——	——	——	——	——	——	——

15

COLLEGE DEGREE IN 3   BY J. WILSON BOWMAN

Financing College

SPIRALING COST OF EDUCATION

Perhaps the most definitive factor in whether or not you will attend a specific school will be financial. As you are well aware, the cost for a college degree is extremely varied. A sampling of universities indicated that over the years the cost of a college education has constantly increased and there is no indication that this trend is going to recede. An example of how the cost of college has increased over the years and how the prices differ are shown in the following chart. As with most costs they continue to escalate, therefore any student planning to enter college today will find the cost to be higher than in previous years.

COLLEGE/UNIVERSITY — Annual Cost

COLLEGE/UNIVERSITY	1977-78	1987-88	2007-2008
Cornell University	6,420	16,320	45,971
Duke University	5,115	14,124	45,121
Harvard University	7,000	17,100	45,620
Northwestern University	6,420	15,636	48,420
Pennsylvania, University of	6,800	16,841	46,124
Stanford University	6,665	16,835	48,420
Smith College	5,935	15,650	45,606
Syracuse University	6,019	13,240	45,608
Tulane University	4,930	15,950	45,550
Yale University	6,950	17,020	45,000

The costs for a college education continue to escalate as much as 20% each year for some schools. Cost varied, from Ivy League Colleges at $45,000; Private at $37,000; to Public at $22,000 in 2008.

Many may feel that the cost of a college education is out of reach. Considering the changes that have occurred in the United States within the last century the problem is far more than the cost of an education, it is indeed the value of a college education. In the 20th century the college education may have been considered a luxury, today businesses are paying for "intellectual property" and a college education is a necessity for anyone planning to be an active participant in the US economy. Granted there are a small number of individuals who "make it" without a college education, it is not the situation for the majority of those who are active participants in the economy. College is expensive but there is assistance in meeting the cost. Once you have selected a college, check the school's Web site for up-to-date information on cost.

Recent data indicates that, for a great number of students, getting a traditional four-year degree is taking five to six years. This additional time will add thousands of dollars to the expense of going to college. After reviewing some of the reasons for this phenomenon it appears that not only could this extra time be avoided, but that with proper planning the additional time and expense could be shaved from the typical four-year requirement as well.

FINANCIAL AID

Financial assistance is available, however to get help you must seek it out. The search for financial assistance should start early by researching the various opportunities that are available; and developing a list of scholarship options. The scholarship list that has been developed should be evaluated to identify those that fit with the goals established. The college choice you make might well depend upon scholarship support secured and the amount of financial assistance available from the schools initially selected. Whatever the cost, it will be a recurring cost and the assistance must be requested each year even as the cost of college tends to increase annually.

College is an expensive undertaking, but there are a host of resources available to provide assistance. These sources have to be identified and contacted. This process of identifying sources should be started prior to 10th grade and contact should be started by eleventh grade. The funds are there but it does take research to find the sources. One Florida A&M student, who knew that her family could not afford the cost of a college education, started identifying financial resources in 9th grade. By the time she reached the 12th grade she had identified and qualified for more than three hundred thousand dollars in financial assistance. Some of the funds for which she qualified required attending certain colleges, others for specific majors. Despite the requirements, she was able to actually secure enough money to completely cover the cost of her college education.

More than fifty billion dollars are available annually for student aid. These funds are from the federal and state governments, local charities, employers, and a host of other organizations. The bureaucracy of student aid can be complicated, but financial assistance is available. Obtaining it requires persistence and commitment. Most colleges have **a financial aid assistant** or director to help students in their search and request for funds. This person's primary job is to work with each student to put together a financial package.

There are basically four areas of assistance:

Grants—awards that do not have to be repaid.

Scholarships—are given by private companies; colleges; local, civic, social organizations; and the National Merit Foundation.

Loans—funds available to cover expenses that require repayment. The payment is generally required to begin nine months after leaving college; either graduation or withdrawal.

Self-help—college work -study, or work opportunities available on campus, for students who qualify based on need.

In order to tap into the numerous financial options the necessary forms and supporting documents must be submitted by the deadlines. Schools participating in the campus-based federal aid programs receive a limited amount of federal funds for each program. Therefore, it is vital to apply by established deadlines in order to be considered for campus-based federal aid, including grants, work-study and low interest loans.

Early in your planning to attend college, you should receive the FAFSA* (Free Application for Federal Student Aid) from your high school counselor. Every student regardless of his or her financial status should complete this form. Completing the FAFSA form requires information that can be used to assess your financial status. It will require information from you and your parents or guardians such as social security number, parent and student tax return, W-2 statements, current bank statements, information on stocks, bonds, insurance, etc. All of this is clearly identified on the forms. Approximately one month after submitting the FAFSA, a Student Aid Report (SAR) will be received from the United States Department of Education. The Federal Student Aid Information Center is available to assist (800–433–3243) in completing the form and sharing information regarding student assistance. This information can be submitted by mail, or online for a quicker response.

College costs include tuition and fees, books, supplies, room and board, transportation, and personal expenses. Tuition and fees are generally non-negotiable while all other expenses are somewhat flexible. Between state, federal, and local programs virtually every student can qualify for some assistance even if it is a loan, regardless of income. Funding that is often overlooked is tuition assistance awarded by local civic clubs, churches, and merchants such as McDonald's. Finding these sources requires some detective work; this search can be aided by checking www.fastweb.com. This site will do a free search on more than 200,000 sources. Therefore, by spending some time on the Internet you should be able to find financial assistance for college.

Federal assistance is available to almost every student through the following aid programs: Pell Grant; Federal Supplemental Education Opportunity Grant (fseog); College Work Study (CWS); Perkins Loans (NDSL – National Direct Student Loan); Stafford Loans (GSL - Guaranteed Student Loan); Parents Loan for Undergraduate Students (PLUS); and Supplemental Loans for Students (SLS).

It is not required that you are an "A" student but good grades do count. To get the needed financial support start early (9th grade is best) spend time at the library or on-line seeking information regarding scholarships and other sources of financial assistance. Develope a plan for financing your education, do not wait until May graduation to begin your search.

21

*FAFSA on the web, *http://www.fafsa.ed.gov/*

FEDERAL GRANT PROGRAMS

Federal Pell Grant—This type of federal assistance is dependent on expected family contribution and whether you are a full-time or part-time student. The maximum award can vary from year to year.

Federal Supplemental Educational Opportunity Grant (FSEOG)—this grant is a federal assistance program for students with exceptional financial need. It is available through the financial aid office at the college. Priority is given to federal Pell Grant recipients.

College Work Study (CWS)—This federal program provides jobs for students. Wages depend upon type of work, skills required and college award program.

FEDERAL LOAN PROGRAMS

Perkins Loan (NDSL)—This is a low interest loan for students with exceptional financial need. It must be paid back after leaving school. The "grace period" before repayment begins nine months after leaving college or graduating.

Stafford Loan (GSL)—two types are available: subsidized and unsubsidized. These are variable low interest rate loans with a defined interest cap. The amount available can increase each year. Repayment is due six months after leaving college or graduating.

> Subsidized Loan is based on financial aid eligibility determined by FAFSA. The government pays interest while student is enrolled, during the grace period and during any authorized deferment periods.

> Unsubsidized Loan is available at any income level. It is not need based. Interest must be paid while in school, during grace period and during any deferment period. Payment of interest can be deferred while in school and during grace periods by adding interest to the principal amount (capitalizing).

PLUS Loan—This is a college loan available from the federal government. It allows parents to borrow sufficient funds to pay for a child's education. Interest rate is variable, depending upon your parent's credit rating. Disbursement is made directly to the school and repayment begins sixty days after the initial disbursement.

The U.S. Department of Education publishes the Student Guide, an annual resource explaining the process for obtaining federal aid. It gives current information regarding student eligibility requirements, deadlines, and borrower rights and responsibilities. Approximately ninety percent of the students attending college receive some financial aid.

The factors that influence a students' ability to receive maximum financial aid are:

Need—the amount of funds actually required based upon family income

Grades—how well the student has performed at high school

Test scores—SAT and ACT (remember these are tests that can be taken more than one time)

School participation—how involved the student has been in school activities

Community involvement—how involved the student has been in community activities

Persistence—ability to continue seeking out sources, follow directions, and meet deadlines.

An important part of the request for assistance is the biographical essay. In addition to the typical document response, the successful biography includes some information that would not appear in any other place. To complete your biography, decide what makes you unique, and highlight those differences. The typical bio should address three distinct parts of your life – past, present, and future. Some information that might be included would be experiences with people whom you consider to have been important in your development; accomplishments, activities and hobbies; your values, personal goals, and contributions you would like to make to the world. The essay should be extremely well done, i.e., have it read by at least three other people including the English professor at your school and be prepared to accept criticism.

Apply for every type of financial assistance for which you qualify. Use loans only as a last resort. Be aware of deadline dates and apply on time to ensure that you will be considered for the maximum assistance for which you qualify.

23

SCHOLARSHIP TRACKING

SCHOLARSHIP TRACKING	Date		Amount of Award	Date		Response
	Requested Info	Rec'd Info		Submit Due	Mailed	
Total						

AWARD LETTER

One final consideration in selecting a college is the financial assistance available. If you have been accepted at one or more institutions, each should have provided you with an award letter, which will indicate the financial support offered. Use the worksheet to compare the offers available at each institution.

Award Letter Worksheet

	College #1	College #2	College #3
College Cost per year	_____	_____	_____
Grants & Scholarships			
Pell Grant	_____	_____	_____
SEOG	_____	_____	_____
State Grant	_____	_____	_____
College Grant	_____	_____	_____
Grant Total	_____	_____	_____
College Work Study Total pay per Year	_____	_____	_____
Loans			
Perkins	_____	_____	_____
Stafford	_____	_____	_____
Subsidized	_____	_____	_____
Unsubsidized	_____	_____	_____
Loans Total	_____	_____	_____
Personal Contributions	_____	_____	_____
Grant Total	_____	_____	_____
Loan Total	_____	_____	_____
Grand Total	_____	_____	_____

24

The First Semester

ADJUSTING TO COLLEGE

If you decide to attend college away from your hometown, and you do not have a friend attending that same college, you may feel like a left handed person in a right handed world. Nothing is familiar, no family or friends—a feeling of foreboding can engulf you and going home may seem like the best option. Hang in there, because all of this will change. You are not the only one who may feel this way. In the first orientation class, just look around. Ninety percent of the people in that room will be feeling exactly the same way. Students just like you will have just left home for the first time. The campus is expecting you; students' arrival is always a momentous occasion. There are several events that are a part of the orientation week.

Some colleges provide freshman seminars and activities designed to help students acquire the knowledge and skills needed to take more responsibility for their learning. If it is available at the school you have chosen, try not to miss this opportunity. It is your first chance to see the new students who will be your classmates. It is probably the last time you will all be together.

The orientation is usually concluded with a campus tour following lectures by staff and a speech by the dean of students or president, and later, a reception. In your tour of the campus, you will be introduced to counselors, meet department heads, and be shown where financial aid and the registrar's office are located. You will be assigned your room and probably get a chance to meet your roommate. It will be a busy week. It is the beginning of the new you—the college freshman, soon to be a college graduate.

Despite these efforts to acclimate students to the campus, little information regarding the real college maze is disseminated. Many students, especially first generation students, find themselves wondering 'what do I do now?' Some of these students find themselves spending the first two years of college trying to figure out what other students came to college knowing, such as how the system operates and how to manipulate it to their advantage. Reading this book will give you that same heads-up advantage.

26

Entering college is the first step toward asserting your independence. Remember high school? The frustration you probably felt about the lack of control over your actions. In college, you will find yourself in nearly total control. You will have the opportunity to make most of the decisions, perhaps even more than you expected and some of which you may find difficult to make. You will decide when to get out of bed, what classes to take, when, if, and what to eat; to clean your room or not to clean it, whether or not to attend class. It is all up to you.

You will select your friends and establish social contacts. There is no doubt that deciding to pursue a college education is a giant step. Your college years can be the most exciting time of your life, filled with challenges and opportunities. The eighteen years of getting to this point in your life have probably not prepared you for all of the challenges you will face. Even though you are away from home, the connection is still only a phone call away. In reality, you might even welcome the fact that you are free at last. With this new found freedom, it is very important that you understand the crucial importance of this first year. It is the determining point for both if and when you will finish school. College costs can range from $10,000 to $40,000 per year; consequently, you can see that the less time spent in college, the more money saved, possibly even enough for a significant down payment on a car.

The assumption is that you are reading this book because you intend to finish college in less than four-years. If this is your goal then you must keep it clearly in focus. Talent and ability are necessary for completing college in three years, however that is not enough. It also requires focus, commitment, persever-ance and time man-ful you need to clarify values. Develop a plan and affirming your that support your ac-yourself succeeding at the goals you set. Work day. Most important is and exhibit a positive ability to be successful. estly see myself in four agement. To be success-your vision and your for yourself recognizing strengths. Create goals tion plan. Visualize the plan you make and toward your goals every the ability to persevere belief system in your ASK: Where do I hon-years? Is college in three years possible? VISUALIZE: Start now to envision yourself as a college graduate in three years!

> **ASK: Where do I honestly see myself in four years? Is college in three years possible?**
> **VISUALIZE: Start now to envision yourself as a college graduate in three years!**

If you have selected a major, great! If not, this must be done before the end of your first year. The main goal is to complete college in less than four-years. To accomplish this, information vital to understanding how colleges are structured and how to negotiate the experience is necessary. There is a difference between the student who is the first in their family to attend college (neophytes) and the students whose parents are college graduates (seasoned students.) The neophyte student, however, must rely on orientation seminars, course catalogues, and student advisors to help guide them through college. Typically, these students find themselves using the first two years at a higher education institution finding out what others come to the college knowing. Seasoned students can draw upon the knowledge and wisdom of their parents to help them navigate the collegiate system. They often receive more guidance and counseling when applying for and getting through college. This book attempts to narrow the gap between the seasoned students and the neophytes.

27

Completing college in three years could be considered similar to the grand slam of tennis, where the French, Wimbledon, US, and Australian Open must be won in the same year. Here the goal is to complete the freshman, sophomore, junior, and senior years of college in one continuous setting taking three years.

PLACEMENT TESTS

Colleges use results from the College Board's Educational Testing Service, a private company that designs and administers these tests, to identify students that will be accepted for admission. These tests should be taken in the 11th or 12 th grade. The major tests are the American College Test (ACT) and the Scholastic Assessment Test (SAT). The SAT is the most widely accepted standardized examination used by many colleges as part of the admission and placement process.

The typical SAT is generally administered on Saturday mornings in established testing centers throughout the United States. It is a three hour examination (but can take up to five hours) with at least six sections. Three Verbal Reasoning sections with 19 sentence completion questions, 40 critical reading questions, and 19 analogy questions; Three Mathematical Reasoning sections, with 35 regular mathematic questions, 15 quantitative comparison questions and 10 grid-in questions.

Eliot Schrefer, an elite SAT tutor, says that writing sections graders are allotted three to five minutes per essay. Therefore, it is important to use the entire two pages given for the essay and be especially aware of and use evidence of sophisticated punctuation – such as semicolons or dashes. He also says if in the reading section you get a question about a passage's main purpose, you can find the main theme in the beginning or the end of the passage.

Successfully completing the mathematics sections requires careful review. Simple errors can make the difference. Before selecting a response, REREAD and REFLECT on the question. Does the answer that you have seem logical?

When applying to a college, it is important to identify the test required (SAT or ACT) and the deadline for receiving test scores. For some colleges, time is of the essence when receiving test results. This information is one of the items used in making student choices.

In addition to the SAT and ACT test used to select students, once admitted, colleges generally administer placement examinations to all incoming freshmen. The results will reflect skills developed in high school. This examination is used to determine the level of initial classes you can participate in the first semester; therefore, it is important in accomplishing your grand slam goal of completing the degree in less than four-years. Many students do poorly on these tests because of lack of preparation and the stress of the entire process. To be prepared for the assessment, review math and vocabulary the summer before entering college. Failure to pass these two tests can result in having to take remedial math and English. However, if passed at a high level it is possible to test out of several typical freshman classes, which can reduce the number of credit hours necessary for graduation by as many as ten to fifteen. In this case you will have an opportunity to move to second level English and mathematics courses and directly into your major. If you are not successful on the test, do not despair. Taking these basic courses in the first semester can get you up to speed and prepare you to be successful in future college classes

REQUIRED SKILLS

Some of the skills necessary for success in a contracted time frame in an academic setting include:

• Knowing how to learn • Competence in computations • Competence in reading • Competence in writing • Time management • Skills in oral communication • Skills in listening • Skills in problem solving • Skills in negotiations • Skills in team participation

Getting the most out of the experience and moving successfully through the experience will depend upon your ability to:

• Work in a diverse environment • Understand the rules and regulations of the college • Be proactive in addressing problems • Build relationships with faculty members • Build peer relationships • Know your student advisor • Be a manager of your time.

CHALLENGES

Remember, you are on your own and as a recent high school graduate that can be an awesome responsibility. There are resources that can assist you but it is up to you to locate and connect with these resources. In addition to the skills that are necessary, there are challenges that may impact your success in college, some of these include, but are not limited to:

- Adjustment to college • Separation from home • Loneliness • Financial problems • Lack of focus on a major • The ability to make friends • Inability to manage time • Understanding course requirements • Difficulty with classes • Attention to safety

NOTES

Planning For Success

BEING SUCCESSFUL

Successful people tend to have very specific qualities: they plan, set goals, have a disposition to work, monitor progress, and use affirmations. You need to develop these techniques or refine them if they are already a part of your repertoire. Take time out each day to close your eyes and see your goals as though they have been accomplished—visualize your success. In order for you to be successful you have to think and talk about your goals as though you have already achieved them. Many successful Olympians are known to have visualized themselves as winners.

Completing college in less than four-years requires a plan – a focused agenda with three main components:

• An identified **major**   • A three year **plan**   • A three year **schedule**

SELECTING A MAJOR

Most colleges offer majors that have a prescribed set of courses, or requirements, totaling between 120 and 150 semester hours to be completed in eight semesters or 12 quarters in four-years. If you begin with a declared major, it is possible to start completing the requirements right away.

If you are one of the lucky few who knows exactly what you want as a major, half of the battle is already accomplished. If not, do not despair. Many students who think they have settled on a major change after the first year. This is probably because they were not really clear about the choices available until after that first year. Consequently, there are some important things that should be considered in making the choice that will probably lead you to your life's work. Key among these is realizing who you are and your life plan.

Understanding yourself will help you in deciding on a major. This is important because selecting a major is often associated with getting a job. Therefore, think about the field you want to work in and your major as a way of reaching that career goal.

32

First, as you think about a major, consider the following:

• Throughout high school, what was your best subject? • What do you enjoy doing? • Do you prefer working with people, ideas, things, or data? • Are you concerned about earning a lot of money or making a difference in your community?

Second, identify your vocational aspirations. In other words, what jobs would you like to have:

• The advantages and disadvantages. • Your ability to achieve success in that area. • The typical demands of that particular choice. • The various jobs that fall under that field.

Third, if you think you have settled on a major, ask yourself:

• What social satisfaction does the proposed occupation offer? • Do you feel passionate about that type of work? • Does it reflect your academic strengths? • Does it reflect your interests? • Is it related to future career options?

The goal is to select a major that leads to a vocation that you will enjoy and can share in the fullness of life. This is the true measure of a successful career choice. Once you think that you have identified a major, run it through Tests I and II below to see if it is still your best choice.

TEST I. WHAT IS MOST IMPORTANT?

Which of the following are the most important to you?

Compensation—security, benefits, salary, recognition, flexibility

Environment—outdoors, pleasant indoor office, factory, warehouse, shop, travel

Responsibility— authority, supervision, freedom, low stress, variety, decision making, few decisions, community service

Working with—animals, people, children, senior citizens, machine, computers, or independently

( ) Compensation _____

( ) Environment _____

( ) Responsibility _____

( ) Working with _____

TEST II. HOW DO YOU LEARN?

What is your learning style?

Analytical – seeks facts, less interested in people, more interested in ideas and concepts, data collector, thorough and industrious.

Creative – likes variety and change, action oriented, learn by trial and error.

Observer – learns by listening and sharing ideas, interaction, interested in people.

Realistic – what is it for, from fact to function, hands on?

( ) Analytical _____

( ) Creative_____

( ) Observer _____

( ) Realistic_____

The question is, "what is important in both life and career?" After taking an inventory of the items above, how important are such things as - where do you want to live? What type of car do you want to drive? What income do you think you will need to support your anticipated lifestyle? In order to get what you want, you need to know what you want. The first step to accomplish this is to know yourself. It is important to identify your strengths and weaknesses to help you decide how you will spend your time in college and in life.

If by chance money is a deciding issue, here is a look at the average 2008 starting salaries from the National Association of Colleges and Employers, Monster TRAK, CareerBuilding.com, Bureau of Labor Statistics.

Visual & Performing Arts	$35,073
English	35,453
Liberal Arts	36, 715
Business Administration/Management	46,171
Economics	51,062
Computer and Information Science	58,677
Chemical Engineering	63,773

Still not ready to make a selection?

Selecting a major is primary to completing college in less than four years. If you are still searching and have not decided on a major, don't panic. The first year at most colleges require that you take general education courses which include classes such as, English, Literature, Mathematics, and Social Studies. However, you should decide on whether you would obtain a Bachelor of Arts or Sciences. This will determine some of your first and second year requirements. If you do not select a major the first year it may be necessary for you to either take more than the recommended number of credit hours during the remaining years at the college, enroll in summer school, or both. Most undergraduate students are required to take a common core of classes that may vary from 20 to 40 credit hours. A careful selection of these courses is important in getting a head start with the required curriculum. Regardless of the major you select, the first-year core requirements should be acceptable for your BA or BS degrees.

If it takes more than one semester (or two quarters)

As mentioned earlier, some students enter high school knowing they will attend college and what they will major in. Then there are others who take one semester, some who take a year, and still others take as long as two years to decide on their major. If you have varied interests there are a few general majors that will allow you to study a variety of subjects within an interdisciplinary studies program or that allows you to design your own major, such as Evergreen State College in Olympia, Washington. To finish college early, the major must be selected during your first year at college. By deciding on a major it is much easier to establish a plan of action that will result in the quick, successful completion of college. Use your major to develop a schedule and an action agenda. The sooner you can create an action agenda, the sooner you can achieve your goals.

Assistance with making a selection

Campus Resources

Each campus has a counseling office or career planning center that is designed to assist you in selecting a major. Visit the career counseling office in the first couple of weeks once you get settled on campus. Request copies of the Occupational Outlook Handbook, Guide to Occupational Exploration, the Dictionary of Occupational Titles or visit the web site *http://www.bls.gov/oco/* for a copy of hiring forecasts in various fields from the Bureau of Labor Statistics. These publications will list all of the occupations that are available in the United States, and will contain an exhaustive listing with far more choices than you can imagine. While at the career center, request to take one of the aptitude or psychology tests, such as the Myers-Briggs. Tests like this one can identify your personal strengths and can assist you in choosing a major based on your personal preferences. Additionally, many colleges have a computer system with access to an interactive career search program. Find out if your campus has one; if so, use it. This resource could possibly identify some choices that you have never considered.

Informal Interviews

With serious commitment to this task, one or two choices for a major should emerge. It would be extremely helpful to identify someone in the field of your choice for an interview in order to get some perspective on the profession, and evaluate your decision. Finding that person might be a chore depending upon the choices you have identified. If you do not know anyone in a particular occupation, meet with your college advisor, consult the librarian, and use the telephone directory, the employment office, or the chamber of commerce. Ask around to find someone who is in that profession. Feel free to call someone you do not know and ask them to share with you information about the choice you have made. Most people will enjoy talking to you about their careers. Before you call, prepare questions and be aware of the time needed for your informal interview. You can also research the career field on-line. Your objective is to learn the options for career paths, the actual preparation required, and what work is involved in the profession.

Family and Friends

Your search should be well underway by the time you head back home for the holiday break. Consult with people in your town who may be working in the field that you have identified. Talk with family, guardians, close friends—people that probably know you better than you know yourself. Share your choices with them to get their impressions of how you might fit in the field you have selected. Remember, these are the people who have known you throughout your growing years. They have watched you develop into a college student. Their input can be extremely helpful as you struggle with the choice of a major. However, do not let yourself be pressured into a career of anyone's choosing on the basis of his or her own values. Make a choice that you can live with. The steps recommended here are those basic to any problem solving situation:

1. Identify the decision to be made
2. Gather all available information
3. Identify the alternatives
4. Evaluate the alternatives
5. Select from among the alternatives
6. Review and evaluate your decision

What if after you have completed the exercise and feel comfortable with your decision, the major doesn't exist? Then you may have to design a major.

If you can identify at least three possible career paths, you can evaluate each based on the decisions you have made, your priorities and information obtained from the sources you have contacted. Information to complete column 2(most important) comes from test 1 (page 33). In column 3, 4, and 5 indicate which of the choices identified best fits what you consider most important. If you can't make a choice from the available options then consider designing a major, keeping in mind the things you have identified as important.

EVALUATING CAREER OPTIONS

Considerations	Most important?	Choice #1	Choice #2	Choice #3
COMPENSATION				
Security				
Benefits				
Salary				
Recognition				
Flexibility				
ENVIRONMENT				
Outdoors				
Office				
School				
Factory				
Shop				
Warehouse				
RESPONSIBILITY				
Authority				
Freedom				
Low Stress				
Community Service				
Variety				
Supervision				
Prestige				
WORKING WITH				
Animals				
Children				
Computer				
Machines				
Adults				
Senior Citizens				

37

DESIGNING A MAJOR

If after extensive research you have definitely settled on a major that is not offered, do not give up! Remember, there are always options; you simply have to refine your plan. Some colleges allow students to design unique majors that fit their specific interest. Even colleges that do not have a formal process for individualizing majors can allow combinations that are logical and coherent. Contacting the right person with the right attitude can create exceptions; start with the Dean of Instruction or the Dean of Students.

If all of this fails, you may have to select a major similar to your original choice. Remember, data indicates that the average person in the United States pursues five different careers in the course of a lifetime. This is due to a shift in values, talents, interests, and opportunities. In view of this fact perhaps the very best major, for the undecided or if the major selected is not offered, would be Liberal Arts.

> *"Decision making is the most important activity– through making choices we create our own lives."*
>
> Kierkeggard

The skills and knowledge developed through the Liberal Arts major can prepare the student to create an effective career and to pursue a vocation that is more than just a job. Such a major would allow the student to select from among many different occupational options as interests change and new opportunities become available. The danger here is having such an eclectic array of courses that it might take more than four-years to graduate. Therefore, if you decide to go this route it is imperative that you work with an advisor to obtain a course audit. To ensure its validity have it signed by the registrar, dean, or division chair. This is your contract with the institution indicating that the courses which appear on the audit represent the complete list required for the degree.

Now that you have selected a major, the most important document is the college cataloguee. It provides the campus philosophy, the expectations and requirements for graduation. It may also provide information on the kind of financial aid that is available.

THE THREE YEAR PLAN

Once your major has been selected the next step is to thoroughly review the catalogueue. This publication contains the rules, regulations, and a description of each class that is offered. It will aid in academic planning, identify the classes required for each major and give the requirements to earn a degree. The catalogueue is vital to establish an educational plan (action agenda) for completing college in less than four-years. Some colleges distribute a catalogue each year and others, every two years. This catalogueue, in effect when you enrolled, represents your contract with the college. Throughout your tenure at the college, curriculum changes will occur. However, as long as you have an uninterrupted tenure at the college, you are only responsible for those courses that were in the original contract (the catalogueue in place when you initially enrolled at the college). Hang on to this catalogueue for as long as you are enrolled. Keep two copies of it and the signed list approved by the registrar, advisor, and department chair. One copy should be for your file and one placed in your most secure place, like a safe deposit box or your grandmother's house. Keep that document somewhere that you know it will always be safe and available.

Developing a schedule is actually relatively simple, but it requires reading the catalogue carefully. Some classes require prerequisites. A prerequisite is a class, usually a basic course that must be completed before moving on to a more difficult course. For instance, you must take Pre-calculus before you can take Calculus. Most instructors will not allow students who have not completed pre requisites to take a class identified as having one. Be sure you take all prerequisite courses your first and second years. Otherwise this could seriously hamper your ability to graduate in three years. It is vital that you know these prerequisites and the sequence in which the classes are offered. All classes are not offered every semester; this makes sequencing very important. Also, be sure to balance easy classes with the more difficult classes. Your schedule will have to be flexible and monitored closely with this in mind. Your plan should be written and include what you want to accomplish in the identified time frame, indicating specifically what is to be accomplished each year. Armed with the list of required courses, develop a year-by-year schedule of courses and the semester they should be completed. Keep in mind the prerequisites you need to complete before taking other courses. Requirements can vary by school, department, and major.

Class Scheduling For Finishing College In Three Years

	FALL		SPRING		SUMMER (IF NECESSARY)	
Year 1	Course	Units	Course	Units	Course	Units
Required General						
Required General						
Required General						
Required Major						
Elective						
Total		18		18		
Year 2	Course	Units	Course	Units	Course	Units
Required General						
Required General						
Required Major						
Required Major						
Elective						
Total		20		20		
Year 3	Course	Units	Course	Units	Course	Units
Required Major 10						
Required Major						
Required Major						
Elective						
Total		20		18		(124)

To ensure that you are on the right track in developing a schedule that will lead you toward a graduation in three years, you must do the following:

1. Identify the entire list of classes required for the major selected.

2. Review the list with your advisor and Department Chair and get a sign-off.

3. Visit the registrar for a final approval and sign-off on the list of required classes.

4. Finally, make three copies of this document and send one copy home for safe-keeping.

Review this document during the spring of each year, in order to make any adjustments necessary due to the availability of class offerings. The schedule should include the classes you need to take in order to meet the requirements of your major, as well as the required general education courses. Meet with your advisor at the end of each semester to review the original audit. This will keep you on track. If you have completed some AP classes during high school they should be used to decrease the number of credits required. It is possible to use as many as 10 AP credit hours in some departments. Courses taken at a local community or city college can also be applied for credit.

41

GRADUATION REQUIREMENTS

The number of credits required for graduation can vary from 120 to 150, depending upon the major selected. Credits are given for the completion of a course and determine one's grade point average (GPA). Courses are assigned a different value and hours are the units that designate time spent in the class. A class that meets for one hour per day, three days a week would be a three-hour course with three unit credits. With satisfactory completion, this class would provide three credits.

Letter grades are used to calculate GPA. The value of grades is as follows: A = 4.0 points, B = 3.0, C = 2.0, D = 1.0. If during the semester, a student takes four, three-hour classes that would equate to 12 credit hours for the semester. If a letter grade of B was received in all four classes, the GPA calculation would be 4 x 3 = 12 x 3 =36; 36 ÷ 12 = GPA of 3.0.

With five three-hour classes the calculation would be:

Class	Grade Value	Credits	Grade Points
Course 1 = A	4 x	3 =	12
Course 2 = C	2 x	3 =	6
Course 3 = A	4 x	3 =	12
Course 4 = B	3 x	3 =	9
Course 5 = B	3 x	3 =	9
Totals		15	48

Total credits received for the semester = 48 divided by the 15 hours taken would equal a GPA of 48 ÷ 15 = 3.2, or approximately B.

In the event that you receive a grade that was not what you had expected, do contact the instructor for clarification. Sometimes mistakes are made in recording and/or reporting grades.

At the end of the semester, each instructor submits letter grades to the registrar. These grades are entered on the student's transcript. All of the letter grades are converted to a numerical score, totaled and the GPA for the semester is calculated. Upon completing the required credits for the degree, the total GPA is calculated. Most colleges require a minimum GPA of 2.0 to award the degree. The GPA is especially important for students who plan to enter graduate school. However, once you have successfully completed college, employers seldom ask about grades or GPA.

Selecting classes

Your decision in choosing classes will most likely fall into one of these four categories:

1. Classes to meet degree requirements
2. Classes for personal interest
3. Classes that are easy
4. Classes to be with friends

The definitive decision should be based on whether or not the course meets requirements for the degree of choice. If they happen to be easy, where a lot is learned, and friends are enrolled, fine! However, the last three should not be involved in the decision to take a particular class. Again you must stay focused on the grand slam in order "to finish in less than four." There is no time for classes that are not on the audit. Review the schedule at the end or the beginning of each semester to ensure that you are on track, prerequisites are met, and that no surprises are on the horizon. All of this is based upon the identification of a major, if at all possible, during the first year.

In The Classroom

MAKING IT IN COLLEGE

Success in the classroom depends upon study habits, attendance in class, and attention to assignments. First, make sure that you know where classes are located, who the teacher is, the books that are to be used in the class, and the exact meeting time. Some students have been known to miss the first class because they could not find the room. This first class can be crucial because it is here that you are given information on class expectations and the grading procedure. These two items are paramount in deciding if it is the class you need to take this semester.

Grades and school go hand-in-hand. I don't think teachers enjoy giving grades. As a professor, I know that it is my least favorite activity. Despite this, students worry about them but they expect them, administration expects them, so teachers give them. You may have left high school with a 4.0 GPA. Do not be disappointed if you are not able to get all A's the first semester. Keep trying; it is still a possibility. If you did it in high school with persistence and commitment you can do it in college. The grades you get will depend primarily on commitment and preparation. For the most part, tests are based upon the kinds of information disseminated during a specified period in a class. Much of what is studied in college will or should be new information. That means time must be devoted to studying this information in order to make it a part of your knowledge base. Osmosis doesn't work. Quiet study time, study groups, and cooperative work groups are some of the various ways to set aside time for studying. It is a guarantee that without dedicated study, grades indicating success will not be received.

REGISTRATION

Registration is a very important part of getting the classes needed in a timely manner. Every college has a scheduled time for students to identify and select the classes they plan to take. Registration appointment time is generally determined by classification (e.g. freshman, sophomore). Classification for registration is based on hours earned, this does not include any credit for courses in which you are currently enrolled. Students may confuse "attempted hours" with hours earned. Know the process! Classes are generally limited to a particular number of enrollees, if you ignore your assigned time it might mean that you will not be able to register for a necessary class until the next semester. Register as early as possible to get required courses and with the teacher of your choice.

Prior to your assigned registration time, check to see if you have any holds on your account. Holds result from payments due, missing signatures, missing transcripts, etc. If there is a hold on your account you will not be able to register. It must be taken care of before you can register.

If it is permissible, consider sitting in on a class that you think you might have difficulty with to get a better understanding of the requirements of the class.

When arranging your class schedule, it would be helpful if you could:

1. Allow time between classes. Avoiding back-to-back classes provides an opportunity, especially the first semester, to review class notes and hand outs. This way you can ascertain the level of comfort you have with the materials disseminated during the class. Another reason to schedule time between classes is because classes scheduled back-to-back generally have the final examinations also scheduled back-to-back.

2. Identify the time of day that works best for you. Are you an early morning person, or do you start to come alive around 10:00 in the morning? You may have the option to select your classes from various time slots, but not always. Understand that every class is not available at every hour and not necessarily available every semester. This is especially true regarding prerequisites, which is why it is important to be aware of your scheduling options. Attending class is definitely a requirement, so plan to schedule classes during times that you know you can attend.

3. Investigate the classes you will be required to take and the professors who teach them. Learn as much as you can about the teaching style of each instructor as it might relate to the techniques with which you feel most comfortable. There are basically five teaching styles that typically characterize the classroom:

   a. Student centered in which the interests and curiosities of the students are the guiding force;

   b. Subject centered, usually a lecture class where content drives all consideration of planning and organization, and the goal is to cover the material as scheduled regardless of the student interest;

   c. Learning centered is typically a balance between student and subject centered styles;

   d. Task oriented in which prescribed lessons are studied and all students are expected to meet established goals within a specified time period;

   e. Cooperative centered where the instructor facilitates the learning experience by encouraging students and directing them as they work in groups.

4. Balance easy classes with more difficult ones. If you can do this, it will eliminate the stress associated with getting through college.

47

Knowing your instructors is as important as selecting classes. Before selecting instructors do a bit of research. Most teachers have some history that might assist in your choice of classes. Look for it. Ask some upper class students about evaluations, which may be available in the department, library, or the dean's office. Look for teachers who:

1. Introduce a variety of techniques in their teaching style, are interested, informed and involved in the subject;

2. Use examples or illustrations to clarify the material, stimulate thinking, and provide active learning opportunities;

3. Present material in an interesting way, and assign work appropriate for the credit;

4. Give tests that are fair, and assign grades fairly;

5. Are helpful when students need assistance; and

6. Are student oriented, and sensitive to students' feelings and problems.

7. You might not find an instructor with all of these qualities. Try for at least 3 out of 6!

48

LECTURES

A majority of college classes are presented as lectures. It is essential to learn how to listen during class lectures. Read and take notes on the topics to be covered in the lecture prior to class. By accomplishing this you will limit the amount of notes that need to be taken during the class and more time can be devoted to listening to comments made by the instructor. If you have taken notes from the readings it will help to focus your attention.

Before the lecture

Research shows that the single force driving most classroom instruction is the textbook. You will need a copy of the text for each class that you take. The textbook is the source, the curriculum guide, and it establishes the calendar and the approach to teaching. Once you have the text, read about the author, the publication date and examine the table of contents. This information will assist you in understanding the messages that are being transmitted to the students and can sharpen your skills as an evaluator as you start to read and understand the goals of the class.

When reading a textbook assignment, the following suggestions could help in your understanding of the chapter and prepare you to be actively involved in classroom discussions.

1. Prepare your note-taking sheet before beginning to read the text book.

2. Each paragraph in the text should have at least one main idea worthy of note. Record this information.

3. For unfamiliar words or phrases - search an online dictionary like *www. m-w. com*.

4. After reading the chapter, formulate at least one question. During class discussion, pay attention to hear if the question is addressed. If the question is not addressed, then you should present the question for discussion. If you are uncomfortable with speaking out, ask the professor at the end of class.

During the lecture

When attending class, take good notes. Some teachers allow tape recorders in class, others do not. If possible, find out if recorders are allowed before going to class. This kind of information tends to be disseminated at the first class meeting. If tape recorders are allowed, half of your work is completed. It is impossible to get every idea on paper so you must carry some of the class lectures in your head. Developing some shorthand techniques for note-taking is essential. If you find that you are not a good listener, learning to listen is a skill that must be developed.

Notes are written for future reference. Don't try to get every word—if you try this, you will miss much of the presentation. When in class, focus your attention on the speaker. Ask yourself what you should learn from the speaker. Listen for main ideas, key words, and points of interest, and then list these. Develop a note-taking format for speedy recording. You can only take good notes if you have read the assignment prior to attending class. This will make in-class recording easier. It is generally from your lecture notes that the test will be derived. Go to class with notes about the topic to be discussed, which can be augmented from the lecture. If you are familiar with the topic being discussed, write only clue words as you listen to the lecture.

When taking notes, use only one side of the note paper; draw a margin about three inches from the left edge of the paper; use the area on the right of the margin to record notes; skip lines to indicate new ideas; practice/develop abbreviations such as w/ for with, etc. as a way to increase speed of note-taking.

Note-Taking Sheet

Key Points	Class Notes	Date

Study Skills

EXPECTATIONS

College is very different from high school. There is a tremendous change in the quality and quantity of work expected. As a college student, you are in a life of self-directed time management. No one will ask, "Did you complete your homework? Is the assignment finished? What time is your first class?" It is strictly up to you. In order to obtain the grades necessary for the grand slam, time must be set aside and devoted to study. Identify a time and place that is right for you, one with limited distractions, not too comfortable but very well lit. Your room is probably not the best place for four reasons: the television, the telephone, other dorm mates and the roommate. Serious study time is vital, identify a spot, make a commitment to be in that space at a specific time each day. A space away from distractions will provide quality time necessary to keep up with assignments. It is much easier to stay on target rather than to play catch up.

CREATE A STUDY SCHEDULE

To aid in planning study options and insure that you get to class on time:

1. Make a schedule of classes to attend.

2. Place this schedule in a visible location in your room.

3. Identify the best time of day for you to study and put it on the schedule.

4. Select a quiet place for daily study (let your room-mate know where it is).

Developing good study skills is crucial in order to complete college in less than four-years. Class, study, test, grade, and instructor are all connected. One follows the other and the grade is the final indicator of whether or not a course has been successfully completed. You may buy a daily planner to schedule your time, or create a simple schedule on your own like the one provided on the next page. Having a schedule is must.

STUDY SCHEDULE

Time	Day	Class / Study Subject	Location
8:00 am	Monday	Study History	Library Carrel
9:00 am		History Class	Room 209, Wilson Hall
10:00 am		Study Economics	Library Carrel
11:00 am		Study Literature	Library Carrel
12:00 pm		Lunch Break	
1:00 pm		Economics	Class Room 70, Barren Hall
2:00–6:00 pm		Work Study	
6:00 pm		Dinner Break	
7:00–8:30 pm		Study Computer Tech	Computer Lab, James Hall
8:00–9:30 am	Tuesday	Computer Tech	Room 160, James Hall
9:30–10:00 am		Break/Snack	
10:00–11:30 am		Literature Class	Room 211, Wilson Hall
11:30 am –12:30 pm		Study Literature	Library Carrel
12:30–1:30		Lunch Break	
1:30-3:00 pm		Study Biology	Library Carrel
3:00–3:30 pm		Break	
3:30–5:00 pm		Biology	Room 117, Hellar Hall
5:00–6:00 pm		Study Computer Tech	Computer Lab, James Hall
6:00–7:00 pm		Dinner	
7:00–8:00 pm		Study History	Library Carrel
8:00–10:00 pm		Social Time w/Friends	

TEST PREPARATION FOR THE CLASSROOM

To be successful in college it is important to learn test taking strategies. Anxiety can be expected at test time—actually a small amount of stress is good, it provides a natural alertness. Keep in mind that the outcome of the test you take can be influenced by your attitude.

When a test has been scheduled, make sure you know where it is to be held and how long it will take you to get there. Be on time, and be prepared. Once in class, listen carefully for directions on the amount of time allocated and how the test should be completed. At the exam site, you can start the test by taking the first five minutes to do a relaxation exercise—close your eyes, take 3 or 4 deep breaths filling your lungs and letting the breath out slowly. This is a quiet exercise that can be done without being noticed.

Here are some additional test-taking tips:
- Wear a watch
- Look over the entire exam before launching into it
- Read all directions carefully
- If directions are unclear, ask for clarification
- Compare the number of questions to the amount of time allotted
- Determine the time available per question
- Pace yourself by carefully monitoring the time allocated for the test
- Highlight the easy questions with a bright marker
- Highlight the more difficult questions with a different marker
- Answer the easy questions first
- Allow time to attempt all items

If there is additional time once you have completed the exam, reread questions to ascertain that the intent of the question was understood, review your responses carefully, make sure that no questions have been skipped, and make changes as necessary.

The textbook can be an extremely useful study tool when preparing for tests, completing class reading assignments, and participating with a study group. Texts are most helpful if the following steps are followed:
- **Skim** the entire chapter to get a **general idea** about the material covered.
- **Read** the **introduction** and **summary** to each chapter. • **Pay particular attention to all visuals, key words, and special notations.** • **Read** the **first line** of each **paragraph**. • **Read** and **answer** the **questions at the end of the chapter** . • **Note** all unfamiliar words and use the dictionary to write the meaning of each. • **Review** all notes relevant to class assignments and all notes before test day.

PRE-TEST STUDY SHEET

Questions / Key words	Chapter focus
1. 2. 3.	1.
1. 2. 3.	2.
1. 2. 3.	3.
1. 2. 3.	4.
1. 2. 3.	5.

SUCCESS ON EXAMS

A plan for success requires knowing your teacher's requirements, attending class regularly, taking resources to class (notebook, calculator, pen, etc.), taking good notes, keeping up with all course work, finishing assignments on time, and finally, preparing for tests. A major part of the academic experience is testing. It is the way teachers are able to determine whether or not students understand the material being disseminated.

Previous Tests

Many teachers place their test from previous semesters on file at the school library or the department library. Find out if they are there and if not where they can be found. Reviewing these old examinations may give a clue to instructor expectations. They can also be found at some fraternity and sorority houses. You must inquire about this because this information is generally not made available to freshmen. It usually takes at least a semester to find this information. Many students never find out about this particular resource. Access to this information can assist you in recognizing the testing style used by the teacher, and serves as an excellent study aid.

Test Options

Success in testing requires that you be thoroughly familiar with the material, know the time frame for the examination, and know how to allocate that time based on the number and type of questions presented. Prior knowledge of the structure or type of the exam will determine study technique to be used.

Typically, examinations are composed of basically two kinds of questions: objective and essay. The major clue to each type of test is to read carefully to understand the specific question that is being asked.

Objective examinations include questions that are multiple choice, true/false, and matching. With objective tests, sometimes items that appear later in the exam may provide information about earlier items. Some of the recommendations for taking objective examinations include:
- Read all items very carefully, anticipate the answer, and then look for it.
- Be sure to consider all alternatives before responding.
- If unsure of an item, skip it.

- After completing the exam come back to items skipped.
- Answer every question if there is no penalty for wrong answers.

Multiple choice   items are composed of two parts. **The stem** – the initial statement and **options** –the available choices. There are two options: the **answer** and the **distractor**. Review all choices and then make an informed guess. There is generally four choices, two are major distractors and are likely to have no relation to the **stem** question. By eliminating these two right away, it gives you a 50/50 chance of getting the correct answer.

- Note whether there are two answers that are opposite.
- Is there is an answer that has a broader application than the rest?
- Are there answers that are grammatical extensions of the stem?

For *true or false*   items, some signals are specific determiners and are useful mainly on poorly constructed test items.
- Words such as *always, never, without exception, only,* often signal false statements.
- Words such as *generally, usually, most of the time,* often signal true statements. The key here is careful reading and understanding the question that is asked. When uncertain select TRUE. There is a ten dency to include more T than F sstatements.Think about it. If there are 50 questions, sheer guessing can yield a score of 25 and studying should significantly increase the score on a true/false test.

With *matching*   questions two lists of items are presented. Items from one list must be identified as associated with an item from the second list. When an equal number of statements and possible answers are presented, try using the process of elimination. Cross out matches that you are certain to be correct, once these have been eliminated, the list is shorter with fewer chances for mistakes. After eliminating the wrong answers make a careful guess from among the remaining choices.

Essay examinations seem a bit more difficult than the objective test but in reality they are straight forward. You can "guess" with the objective test, with the essay test you must have something to say, and to say it well is the mark of a good student. Successfully completing essay tests depends upon understanding the subject vocabulary and the question that is being asked. Key words such as describe, analyze, critique, explain, define (etc.) are often used, and should lead your thought. The method used here should be just as you would use if you were writing an essay. You need an introduction, related statements, and a conclusion. Make sure that you understand the question and know the amount of time that should be allocated for each question. Before starting to answer the essay question—brainstorm, write down all of the things that come to mind about the question, organize this information in a very brief outline, develop a thesis sentence and start writing. This process should take no longer than five minutes before starting to respond to the question. Repeat this process—read, brainstorm, outline, thesis, respond, and move forward—as you move to the next question. If there is time, go back to the beginning and re-read the responses that you have prepared. If the essay question is presented as a "take home" examination follow the same directions above. However, in this case presentation is important; there is ample time to carefully consider your response and the manner in which it will be presented.

Authentic Assessment is a move away from traditional standardized test and criterion-reference tests, ones that use true-false and multiple choice format. It is an inclusive term for alternative assessment methods that examine a student's ability to solve problems or perform tasks that closely resemble authentic situations. There are four components to this assessment format.

1. a reason for the assessment
2. a performance to be evaluated
3. exercises that elicit that performance
4. systemic rating procedure.

This testing type is becoming more prevalent in college classes.

Research Papers and Essays

Much of what is taught in college is how to present ideas in written form. Each person has a different way of approaching the writing process. You must develop one that works best for you. If you do not already have a developed writing process, locate and visit the writing center. There you will find assistance in developing your personal style. The writing center is the place to learn the generally accepted format for citing references when completing research papers. There they can explain the various methods and the one recommended by the campus, whether it's APSA (American Political Science Association), APA

(American Psychological Association), MLA (Modern Language Association) or some other method. Know the style that is recommended by your particular instructor; different instructors may have different styles.

The research paper is basically a group of related paragraphs about one topic. It consists of an **introduction** defining the issue to be addressed, a **body** that presents supporting paragraphs, and finally, the **conclusion**, which represents a summary of the information that has been identified and discussed in the body. The introduction is important because readers decide there whether or not to read further. A good introduction includes the thesis statement which presents an idea that is debatable or needs explanation. The body presents supporting paragraphs backed up by research, ideas that prove or explain the thesis idea. The number of paragraphs depends upon the topic selected and ideas that must be explained. Typically each paragraph has two parts, a topic sentence and subsequent supporting details.

Writing a good essay requires four essential steps: prewriting, writing, revising, and editing. Before developing an essay, do some brainstorm mapping. Ask yourself, *what topic am I most familiar with, what can I write about with ease, what do I know?* To start you will need a **thesis statement**, or a sentence that states the main point to be addressed in the essay. This statement helps to focus your brainstorming and might be expanded or revised into an introduction to the essay. Once you settle on a topic, list all of the things that come to mind as you consider the topic. Do some quick research on the Internet about the ideas you've brainstormed. Group both the brainstormed and researched data into an **outline**. Use the outline to develop a statement that can be used in a working draft. This unifying statement can be the basis for the introduction to your essay. To make the outline:

- Brainstorm and research a list of details
- Group related details
- Identify a heading for each group
- List related details under each heading
- Determine the order for each grouping

The thesis statement and the outline are used to write two possible introductory paragraphs for the essay. Decide which paragraph identifies the topic, indicates the main point, and predicts the content and organization of the essay.

The **introduction** might begin with a question, an incident, a contrast or comparison, a general statement, or background information. The **body** of the essay contains the expanded outline in sentence and paragraph form. Each main heading in the outline will become the topic sentence of a paragraph. The details under the heading will become supporting sentences.

Restate your main point in the conclusion, which is intended to help the reader remember the main point and to give closure to the essay. Read, re-read, expect to revise, and edit the initial draft. As stated earlier, a really good paper will require at least four rewrites. In preparing a research paper, it will require that you draw upon work that others have completed. When you use the work of others, you must give credit to the author. Failure to do so is plagiarism.

Plagiarism (copying the work of another author and claiming it as your original work) *is a dir ect path to being expelled* . Don't do it! There is no other way to put it. Many students find themselves pushed against the wall when it comes to completing written assignments and they attempt to take the easy way out. It does not pay off. Start papers when they are assigned, instead of putting it off. Time seems to fly when it comes to completing assignments. Be proactive and make maximum use of your time. There is much more time available if you work from the point when assignments are given, rather when they are due.

THE SCHOLAR'S TOOL: WORDS

The better command you have of words, the greater your chance to pass easily through college. The English language is composed of more than a million words. As a college student, you should have a working knowledge of at least 100,000 words. Throughout your college experience, you will continue to amass a host of new words. You should not leave this to chance; learn new words each day. Focus on adding to your current vocabulary, and you will significantly increase your status as a college graduate. Some words are included in the appendix of this book for your perusal. Do not limit your quest to these few words; use the dictionary on a regular basis. You can even get a friend to join you in a challenging and competitive game of learning new words.

Vocabulary is often an overlooked component when getting into and being successful in college. If you have read widely, chances are your word power is well developed. If you have not, then it is vital that you broaden your vocabulary in order to do the kind of inquiry thinking required for success in higher education. Any scholarship test that you will be required to take will have vocabulary as a major component. Your vocabulary will influence how well you do on the English placement, which will in turn determine how quickly you can accelerate through your required English classes.

If you decide to improve your word skills, select a vocabulary guide that teaches how to discover word meaning from context, words derived from foreign languages, and how to recognize words from derivatives. Reading, writing, listening, and speaking will all enhance your vocabulary.

As your vocabulary is being built it is very important to understand the role that roots play—the root is the basic part of a word. Most of our roots come from Latin and Greek therefore, learning the roots can increase knowledge of unfamiliar words. Knowing prefixes can immediately give one access to a family of words. By knowing prefixes, you will open up a huge number of words that can be added to your vocabulary. Additionally, there is a set of words that should be part of a college graduate's repertoire (see appendix).

STRESS MANAGEMENT

Testing is an unavoidable part of the college scene, and is a major cause of stress for college students. To complete an examination with the best possible results and to decrease the stress associated with testing, preparation is necessary.

Stress is often associated with feeling a lack of control. With preparation, you move to a position where you can feel in control. When you have completed the exam remember, it is just one test, and there will be others. If you have done your best, that is all that can be expected. Stress is mental and controllable. A few suggestions to avoid stress are:

- Plan to spend at least two nights studying for any major examination.

- Avoid falling behind in one class, while concentrating on another.

- Keep up with assignments and work ahead in classes as much as possible.

College can be stressful and the freshman year, with so many new experiences can be a primetime for stress. It may cause emotional and physical problems that may damage both your health and performance.

Excessive worry can trigger the physical sensation of headaches, anxiety, insomnia, and tense muscles. This is often evident whenever the thought of preparing an assignment, taking a test, completing a report, or meeting a deadline approaches. This can lead to absenteeism, diminished memory, increased errors, lack of concentration, and on, and on. Each individual will have different ways of handling stress associated with being a college student. The important thing is to recognize that stress is a part of the college experience and it requires that you develop techniques for handling college life in a manner that allows you to meet your responsibilities. Being successful in college is associated with being present in class. It is imperative that you recognize those situations that impact your well being and can interfere with class attendance.

You move away from home, you are making adjustments to a new environment with a diverse group of people; time requirements may be unlike any you have had to deal with before; adjustments, assignments, tests, reports, so may things to do and so little time.

On campus there are three places where you can find help in coping with stress: the counselor's office, the health center and the library, where you can locate a host of resources with techniques for handling stress.

Most resources will recommend some simple ways stress can be managed:

- Changing thoughts about responsibilities and activities such as tests, assignments, deadlines;
- Understanding the importance of planning to avoid stressful situations;
- Taking care of yourself physically by eating properly;
- Getting adequate sleep and learning to relax.

In stressful situations, some relief may be achieved by:

- Stopping what you are doing to take a break;
- Taking time out of all activities to relax;
- Changing the environment—go for a walk, take a shower, clean a closet;
- Practicing meditation.

MEDITATION

In preparation for an examination—one of the more stressful events during college—try meditation, a method of relaxation designed to reduce stress. There has been much research that recommends meditation to relieve stress. Meditation can bring calm and tranquility and enable you to approach examination time in a more calm and relaxed state of mind. The great thing about meditation is that anyone can do it. There are many meditation techniques. Here is one method involving simple meditation steps based on focusing:

Preparation for Meditation

1. Set aside a time when you can be free from interruptions
2. Wear loose, comfortable clothing
3. Choose a quiet, peaceful place
4. Play music, low and soft

Meditation

5. Sit in a comfortable spot, on the floor, or in a straight chair, etc.
6. Breath normally, but focus on the rhythm of your breath
7. Breathe slowly, deep and regular; count exhaled breath from 1–10
8. Close your eyes and be aware of the air entering and leaving your body
9. After three minutes open your eyes and take in the sights and sounds around you.
10. Repeat 7 and 8 for 3 sets of 3 minutes each.

After Meditation

11. Rise slowly
12. Resume normal activities
13. Session time should gradually increase
14. Start with 10 minutes sessions; build to 20 minutes.

The aim of meditation is to free the mind of all distracting thoughts and to achieve a calm relaxed state. This does not require excess time and can be extremely helpful.

VITAL RESOURCES:

The Library

Become very familiar with the library. It is virtually impossible to complete college successfully without spending time in the library. Research papers, term reports, etc. all require time in the library. The computer is a great resource but it alone will not satisfy most professors. The college library is an incredible resource. For every assigned text book, there is a similar text that may present a different view of the topic, or may be better written with easier explanations than the one selected by the instructor. Do not rely on your textbook as the end all. Chances are that the teacher is using a text that was popular when they attended college, or they are using a newer version instead of an older one with better explanations. Find a book on the same topic that you enjoy reading. Believe me, there is one in the library.

Identify a time and place that is right for you. Choose a location with limited distractions that is not too comfortable, but is well lit. Your room is probably not the best place for the following reasons: television, your roommate, other dorm mates, and your bed. Find a space that is right fo you and make a commitment to be in that space at a specified time each day. A space away from disractions will provide the concentration time necessary to keep up with your assignments. Remember to turn your cell phone off. It is much easier to stay on target rather than to play "catch up". In order to stay on top of work required, keep a daily log of all assignments, tests, reports.

The Study Group

For some classes, establishing a study group might be a good idea. This provides an opportunity to get various views on the test topics and it can expand your understanding of the subject. Generally, groups are composed of class members who can find a common time to meet and discuss class notes. If you join or form a study group, make sure that it consists of serious goal-oriented students who are committed to successfully completing their education. A study group can be a vital component in making it through the college maze. For new freshmen students, identifying, forming or joining a study group can be an awesome task. The question is where do you start? The most likely place to start a study group is within the class. Identify some students who are serious about being successful and make the suggestion. Simply ask "are you interested in having a study group?" There are only two possible answers – yes or no. Believe me, you have just asked the question that at least three others wanted to ask, but were hesitant to do so. Establish a meeting time and place – those who meet on time with text books and notes are the ones who are interested and serious. A study group continually provides an opportunity to extend the class session but in a smaller less stressful environment. The different study habits of members of the group would provide an alternative view of the topic that had been introduced in the class. With a study group the opportunity to approach a topic discussed in class from different directions is provided. The study group also offers some distinct advantages to studying alone if it is a well-defined group.

First Year Challenges

LIFE AS A COLLEGE STUDENT

The first year in college is about separation from home, family and friends. It's about learning to live in an environment unlike any previous situation. It is the first step to adulthood—the first chance for you, as a student, to be "on your own." The college scene can be chaotic, exciting, and quite overwhelming. This has been the case for thousands of students, and most have been able to handle the responsibilities that come with freedom. Others have returned home only to go back to school at a later time in life. Some quit for good and others have started successful careers without a college degree.

There are several typical situations not specifically related to academics that can or might be problematic in your first year. These include managing time, finances, and classes, as well as your relationships with roommates, new

" friends", and associates.   As a new student you will have a host of decisions to make without a lot of support. It is imperative that you develop skills of coping and problem solving. Success in college depends upon refining these skills. As with any problem, there is more than one solution but you must first know what the problem is and be able describe it. Once the problem is identified, brainstorm on every possible solution you can conceive. Then evaluate the solution that you believe to be the most feasible, or the one that is easiest to live with. Consider everything that is involved in that solution, and write it all down. Now do the same for one or two other solutions, and compare and contrast the options until you find the best option. Once you think you've found the best solution, implement it. If it doesn't work, go back and start the process again. This time you'll have a better handle on the problem. Remember, some problems can be avoided simply by managing your time better.

LEARNING THE CAMPUS COMMUNITY

An important bit of information in moving from home to a college campus is realizing that college is a community of diverse individuals, probably unlike any other community in which you have lived. Though it is primarily a place to learn and grow, it will have both positive and negative aspects, and you must be safety conscious. College campuses have accidents, crime, injuries, assaults, rape, burglary, theft, vandalism, auto theft, and other crimes. Though the campus administration is concerned about the safety of each student, your personal awareness and involvement is also very important because it can provide some safety to other members of the community.

To maintain your comfort level in this new community, consider taking the following steps:

1. Using common sense in all situations is your best bet.
   a. If you must walk in the evenings, walk with a friend. Some campuses have organized companion systems.
   b. Always walk with purpose. This displays a sense of strength and confidence.
   c. Avoid isolated areas—day or evening.
2. Take a course in self-defense.
3. Always be aware of your surroundings.
4. Be alert for your safety and avoid hazardous environments.

      a. Know location of fire escapes, fire doors.

      b. Location of fire extinguishers, alarms, and smoke detectors.

5. Know proper emergency procedures and phone numbers for assistance.

6. Be aware of fire safety rules and remember fire can start from:

      a. Cigarettes

      b. Candles

      c. Decorations

      d. Space heaters

      e. Hot plates

      f. Irons

      g. Curling irons or curlers

TIME MANAGEMENT

The trouble with being "free at last" is knowing how to control the time that you have. Time does fly, especially when you are not paying it any attention. Every one has the same amount of time, but how it is used makes all the difference. We tend to use the time we have, without considering how effective we are in its use.

Time management is influenced by the value that is attributed to the things that have to be accomplished. Perhaps more than anything else, how you manage your time will determine your success in college.

As a new student, so many new things will present themselves and will require that you make a decision:

- To join or not to join?

- To party or not to party?

- To skip class or to attend?

- To sleep in or to get up?

There will be so many choices on how to spend your time. How you use your time will be critical in accomplishing your goal of completing college in less than four-years. Think about it. Everyone in college has exactly the same amount of time. No more, no less. The difference in those who are successful and those who are not will depend upon how time is managed.

69

If you are not used to managing your time, then you are in for a big shock. Classes generally operate between 8:00 am and 4:00 pm. Activity classes and laboratory classes are usually held in the afternoon and can go as long as 5:00 or 6:00pm. Some colleges offer evening classes, which extend the school day until 9:00 or 10:00 pm.

In order to accomplish all that is to be completed in a timely manner, you will probably need a *daily planner* . You may become a time watcher until your body is programmed to meet your various time commitments. One of the difficulties of time management is establishing priorities, which are directly linked to your obligations and goals. If your goal is to complete college in the least amount of time, then you must realize that your amount of discretionary time is extremely limited. Therefore, becoming heavily involved in extracurricular activities must give way to time on academic tasks. This, of course, does not suggest that extracurricular activities should be avoided. But it does mean you should carefully evaluate all of the activities and organizations you consider joining.

It is important to have time to relax and get to know other students. To best meet your objective, it would be a good idea to get involved with activities that are intellectually oriented, in line with your values and goal system, and related to your selected major.

As you get started with the daily planner, consider all the things that you have to do between the hours of 7:00 am and 11:00 pm. Enter all classes and activities into your schedule or daily planner. Review the schedule to ensure that adequate time has been allocated to class attendance, studying for each class, and self-time such as sleep and recreation. It might be helpful to use color highlighters to identify special activities and the time allocated. Make sure that your schedule includes the amount of time required, or that you intend to allocate, for each task. Try this for one week, making adjustments when needed; the idea is to establish a routine of activities and time utilization that can be consistently followed. Note any special requirements for class or other commitments. Schedule everything: tests and examinations, due dates for reports, special speakers, any required off campus events, even special activities and social commitments.

Keep in mind that some time must be allotted for self-time. This could include participating in the campus activities that can be a welcome escape from the rigors of study. Also allow time to meet new people and become acquainted with the college campus environment. Most colleges offer an outstanding number of opportunities for involvement. If you can identify an organization that is right for you, you may want to consider joining. Extra-curricular activities are an important part of the college experience. Decide the amount of time you want to devote to each activity, keeping in mind that you only have a specified amount of time. Once you feel comfortable with the time identified to be spent on study, work, recreation, and activities, transfer this information to your daily planner.

To get a handle on time management, make a list of the ways you use your time and then evaluate your time usage. Be sure to block out areas for every category: class attendance, study, personal, sleep, etc. Do not overlook any of your activities. Everything must be listed so that you can see how your time is actually spent. Complete the chart for at least one week. This way you can identify the time required for most of your activities. Completing a week of time sheets is about the only way to get a true picture of the amount of time that is being devoted to studies. Remember, success in college is directly related to the amount of time spent on studies. You do not want to over book yourself, but you do want to accomplish tasks in a timely manner.

The maximum day is 24 hours. Students need at least 7 hours sleep/8 hours would be better. This leaves 16-17 waking hours, successful people use these hours wisely.

SCHEDULE YOUR DAY

How does your day shape up? It can make the difference between success and - - -

Time	Activity	Personal	Study	Fun	Other
6:00 am					
6:30 am					
7:00 am					
7:30 am					
8:00 am					
8:30 am					
9:00 am					
9:30 am					
10:00 am					
10:30 am					
11:00 am					
11:30 am					
12:00 pm					
12:30 pm					
1:00 pm					
1:30 pm					
2:00 pm					
2:30 pm					
3:00 pm					
3:30 pm					
4:00 pm					
4:30 pm					
5:00 pm					
5:30 pm					
6:00 pm					
6:30 pm					
7:00 pm					
7:30 pm					
8:00 pm					
8:30 pm					
9:00 pm					
9:30 pm					
10:00 pm					
10:30 pm					
11:00 pm					
11:30 pm					
12:00 am					

Identify how your time is being used and whether it was for a personal activity, or in class, studying alone or with a group, or at a non class related activity=fun, the last column is for any activity that does not fit in the first three boxes.   Example:

Time	Activity	Personal	Study	Fun	Other
6:00 pm	Cafeteria	x			
6:30 pm	met with study group		x		

FINANCIAL MANAGEMENT

Credit cards figure heavily in managing finances. The acceptance of admission to college generally comes with a credit card offer. Some parents provide students with a credit card on their account. This is an awesome responsibility. However, because it is on the parent's account it provides an opportunity for the account to be reviewed regularly. Some parents make the mistake of giving the card and allowing the student total responsibility. One parent that I know gave their daughter a credit card on her account. The student made purchases and for a while kept up the payments. The parent stopped monitoring the account. When the parent made an effort to use the card, she found that the card was in default because the payments had not been kept up and a negative report was put on the parent's credit score. It took more than three years to remove that negative information from the parent's report. Easy access to ATM machines and credit cards can really be a problem for an individual who has counted the number of checks in mom's check book as an indication of available money in the bank.

> *"I got my first credit card as a college student. This was a big mistake. It was so easy to go over the limit and make only the minimum payment on my account. It has taken me years to pay off that credit card. If only I had realized the value of maintaining good credit earlier in life."*
>
> Kim McAfee

Typically, acceptance at a college is the trigger for receiving a credit card. Corporations expect to have you as a lifetime customer. Keep in mind you have no job, except perhaps work study, and yet you are offered a credit card. This should make you skeptical. A credit card with a $3,500 limit is, in reality, a bill that could last for a significant part of your life. It might start with an interest rate of less than 5%. However, in time it can climb to more than 22% if you are

73

ever late paying a bill or go over your credit limit. This could mean that the monthly payment on the account which started at something like 15 to 25 dollars could jump to as much as 55 - 60 dollars a month. If a credit card is in your future, each month read the bill to understand how interest rates can vary and the relationship between recommended payment and the monthly decrease in the card balance.

Do not use cash advance, stay within your credit limit, and do not charge more than you can afford to pay. Remember, as you use a credit card you have made a LOAN that must be paid back. If you do decide to use the card remember that your financial goal is focused specifically on getting out of college with the least expense. The card should only be used in case of a true emergency and paid off before any interest is accrued.

In financial planning, what you have on one side is money coming in and on the other is money going out. Just as you set goals for completing college, setting goals related to finances is equally as important. To properly manage the money that has been budgeted for college requires a money management plan. Consider one based on your response to these questions: What sources of funds do I have? Savings, parents, job, scholarship, loan, relatives? When are the funds available? Monthly or on birthdays, Christmas, special occasions? and finally, Where does it go?

Perhaps more important than the source of income, is how income is used. This information is required to establish a financial plan. You must have an idea of: the actual costs that occur monthly? Annually? Now and then? This kind of information can be obtained from a spending record. With this information you can start tracking your spending, and developing a budget, which is the first step in controlling spending. When finances are controlled, it significantly decreases the stress that occurs when a bill is due and there are no funds available.

SPENDING RECORD

Wk.	Sunday	Monday	Tuesday	Wednesday	Thursday	Friday	Saturday
1							
2							
3							
4							

75

This chart should be kept for at least two months to get a more realistic picture of where your money goes. You will be able to distinguish needs from wants. Once this is completed you are ready to develop your college financial plan.

FINANCIAL ASSISTANCE WORKSHEET

Net Income Sources	Annual		Monthly
_____	$_____		$_____
_____	$_____		$_____
_____	$_____		$_____
_____	$_____		$_____
Total Annual Income	$_____	Total Monthly Income	$_____

Expenses

	Annual	Monthly
Food	$_____	$_____
Clothing		
Purchases	$_____	$_____
Laundry	$_____	$_____
Dry cleaning	$_____	$_____
School needs		
Textbooks	$_____	$_____
Note paper	$_____	$_____
Pens/pencils	$_____	$_____
Entertainment/Recreation		
Sports	$_____	$_____
Movies	$_____	$_____
Restaurants	$_____	$_____
Hobby	$_____	$_____
Transportation		
Bus/Metro	$_____	$_____
Gas/oil	$_____	$_____
Maintenance	$_____	$_____
Auto Insurance	$_____	$_____
Credit Card Payments		$_____
_____	$_____	
_____	$_____	$_____
Total Annual Expenses	$_____	**Total Monthly** Expenses $_____
Emergency	$_____	$_____
Savings	$_____	$_____

Living Arrangements

HOME AWAY FROM HOME

The decision to live on campus or off campus is a serious one. Living on campus offers some real advantages. The food might be bad, but someone else is responsible for the grocery shopping, food preparation, and cleaning afterwards. The dorm is not like home, but it is on campus with relatively easy access to classes and the library. It takes care of transportation problems and it keeps you in touch with classmates.

Living off campus also offers some advantages that are worth considering. It gives you an opportunity to be on your own. You have to seriously manage your money to be able to cover rent, utilities, laundry, etc. You have to shop for groceries, cook, and clean. You would probably have more control over noise and visitors, and you would not have to relocate at the end of each year. However, the decision should be carefully weighed to ascertain the benefits of each location. Consider what you want in housing, and then identify the pros and cons of each option.

Housing for the first year should definitely be on campus. Here you meet the people that will occupy the world that you will enter upon graduating. The opportunity to identify people who have the values, personality, and general characteristics that you might want in your friendship chain is available. Living on campus is synonymous with becoming a mature adult; it cannot be replaced. It is the time when you recognize, perhaps for the first time, the experience of living in a diverse community.

ROOMMATES

In some respects, your roommate is your first social partner on campus. Long time friends are replaced by new acquaintances. Even though roommates are an important part of college life, having a roommate can sometimes be touchy. The average dorm room is about the size of a prison cell and has to be occupied by at least two people. If at all possible, try to meet or call your roommate before the beginning of classes to break the ice.

Some decisions can be made before hand to eliminate some of the problems associated with two or more people living in such a small space. In making these decisions, keep in mind that each person will need to be flexible in order for the arrangement to work. Who will pay which bills (especially if you live off campus), how the rooms are to be kept, how loud and how late music is to be played, yes or no to overnight visitors, these are just some of the questions that could be addressed before classes start.

With two or more individuals required to co-exist in an enclosed space - which serves as a bedroom, living room, study, retreat, and playroom - for an extended period of time is expecting a lot. Successful domesticity requires a considerable amount of compromise to avoid mayhem. Living together requires communication, the ability for each person to clearly express any unique sensitivity that (early risers vs. late sleepers). This requires a willingness to hear what characteristics about you might irk others, "opening up" and sharing is required for a healthy living arrangement. However, regardless of how well things are clarified, disagreements will arise when living in such close quarters. This is when problem-solving skills become important.

There is no doubt that dormitory living provides challenges and opportunities for learning and developing problem-solving skills. You might go through college with one roommate or you may have a different roommate each year. If the first year roommate "works," meaning you are able to establish a workable living arrangement, it may be worth it to maintain that relationship throughout your stay on campus. This is not to say that your roommate will be a best friend. Throughout your years at college, you may have a different dorm room each year and a different roommate, who does not have to be your best friend. However, if you are able to maintain a roommate throughout your stay on campus it will eliminate the chore of having to become familiar with another set of habits each year.

OFF-CAMPUS LIVING

Though I am an advocate for living on campus, by the time a student becomes a senior, moving off campus might be a consideration. This offers another step toward entering the adult world, moving away from family and toward the responsibilities of being totally on your own. The down side is that all your meals are your own responsibility, and the campus will probably be farther away from you, including classes, the library, and your friends. Prior to such a move, the following should be considered:

- Distance from campus
- Will it require a car
- Is there public transportation
- Time of the first class
- Access to study group
- Safety
- Price
- Eating plan (on campus or not)
- Roommates
- No roommate

NON-ACADEMIC HURDLES

Adjusting to being away from Home

There truly is, no place like home. Entering college is your open door to the rest of your life, and getting acclimated to being away from home is a necessity. Accept the fact that you may be unhappy in the new unfamiliar environment, maybe even sad and lonely despite the fact that you are with thousands of people every day. Trust me it too shall pass. You cannot allow the fact that you are lonely result in your missing class. As a college student no one will check to see if you are in class. In reality you could stay in bed and not go to class but that is viewed very negatively by professors. Many classes have an attendance requirement; therefore, missing class will impact your grade in that class. It's ok to cry, as a matter of fact, you should miss home and your friends, probably every other freshman is feeling exactly the same way that you do. Cry if you must but keep your eyes on the goal.

Having an Automobile

Certainly having a car puts you in a special position—but a car can be very costly. Most campuses have more cars than parking spaces, and some charge parking fees. In some colleges freshmen cannot have cars. An automobile can be a magnet for time wasting and then there is the problem of being the "dormitory taxi" for all your friends. Unless you are a senior with a necessary job off campus, I would consider a car an unnecessary expense and a major negative. But it is for you to evaluate. What is transportation like around the campus? If you have a car, where will it be parked? What are parking fees? Is it necessary to drive to class? Will you let your roommate drive? If others drive your car how will that affect insurance cost? With gas from $1 - $3/gallon, who will pay for fuel? Maintenance? Will it be an asset in getting back and forth between home and school? If you live off campus, a car may be a necessity, and an extra expense. Most campuses require that freshmen spend at least the first year on campus.

Extra-curricular Activites

Extra-curricular activities are a part of most college campuses. As mentioned earlier, though they are available it is vital that you give them the time that best fits your goal. These activities are of major importance for some students but not for a student who intends to complete college in a limited time. However, with careful planning and following a strict schedule some extra curricular activities can become a part of your prescribed plan. Many institutions have a service learning component associated with certain classes and in the real sense these are not extra-curricular but co-curricular activities. Consider these questions before getting involved:

- How much time will it require;

- Are the activities associated with any of your classes;

- Will it enhance my college experience;

- Will it make a difference on my resume;

- Can it be scheduled without undue hardship on the required classes;

- Will it enhance the quality of my life; is it an activity that will be beneficial to my health?

Consider all of these, always with your goal in mind.

83

Social Connections

FRIENDSHIPS

Be intentional about developing a network of friends with whom you can foster mature healthy relationships. As you settle in and become a part of this new community you will find your place. You are free to make most of the choices that will impact your life on campus. The decisions you make from the first day forward are up to you. During college, you will find out who you are, what your abilities are, and what you value. Relationships that will impact your life will begin in college—some will be lasting, others dissolved. This process consumes time and energy. Whether you recognized it or not, high school was a relatively homogeneous place. As you enter college you will be thrown into a new world, the real world. You will meet people from places you cannot pronounce, you will share living arrangements with people from different ethnic backgrounds, and you will mature.

Identifying a group that is related to your major or intellectual interest would allow for a social outlet as well as keep you focused on your goal. It might also provide an opportunity to get to know people of different cultural or ethnic backgrounds. Try to develop a mix of relationships with positive individuals—some for guidance, emotional support, social integration, intellectual stimulation—that have your best interest at heart. What you do during these years will have an impact on shaping your future.

Whether you try to or not, you will meet many people. Some will become "friends" and others will remain acquaintances. Being likeable depends upon one's ability to be natural while connecting with other people and learning how to express yourself. Be cautious of sharing your life story too soon, and learn to be a good listener. When it comes to social skills, being a good listener is much more important than being wise and witty. Relationships do not always stay the same. A "best friend" does not always stick around as you expected. In a relationship there is a giver and a receiver, but the best relationships enjoy a mutual exchange. Give up trying too hard to be liked, and simply be yourself. Honesty counts for a lot. Try being a leader rather than a follower.

FRATERNITIES AND SORORITIES

Relationships are an important aspect of life and the college experience. Many students meet their future spouse and future employers in college. Fraternities and sororities offer a way of getting to know a group of people. They are usually advocates for campus activities. How these groups are perceived on campus, depends on the campus. Fraternities and sororities do not exist on all campuses; some campuses have never had them; other colleges have dismissed them. Becoming a part of these groups depends upon being invited. This usually does not happen until after the first semester, or first year of college.

Fraternities and sororities are responsible for many of the activities that take place on campus. So being in the swing of things can be influenced by whether or not you are a member of one of these organizations. They can provide entry into extra-curricular activities that can provide an escape from the rigors of study. However, they can also provide a trip down the wrong path, which will not bring you closer to your goal. So check out the organizations carefully before committing to anything.

DATING

There is quite a difference between dating in high school, and dating in college. Students dissatisfied with their high school identification often try to mold themselves into something different in college. Trying to be someone different from the high school person can lead inevitably to frustration. We all want to be liked, and sometimes so much that we try too hard, or we don't try at all. Instead of focusing too much energy on your image, take time to build meaningful relationships. Strong and positive relationships can impact your enjoyment of the college experience and provide support for you as you work toward reaching your goals.

Too often, students with this new found freedom fall "so in-love" that the first year of college is a total disaster. The guy or gal that is the object of their affection may not be as serious as was originally thought, and all the time spent with that person wasted their study time, and now the relationship is history and grades are down. This is especially true of freshmen girls who are wooed by upperclassmen; some of whom are already committed to upper-class girls. Watch out Freshwomen!

In an interview with a sophomore, he shared with me that his first year started off great, but ended very disappointing. The first semester was a breeze. He earned four A's and three B's. Then he met a "fine" classmate and study time decreased while together time increased. At the end of the semester his 3.6 GPA had dropped to 3.0, and he had flunked one class. His parents threatened to move him to another school. At the end of our conversation, he shared that he was still trying to convince his parents that he was seriously committed to his studies and wanted to return to the same college.

Freshmen arrive on campus without a social reputation. In order to ease into the dating scene, group dating might be an option. This way a group of guys and girls get together and go to a movie, a restaurant, some college sponsored event, or out for coffee. A group date is inexpensive, provides an excellent opportunity to get to know people without any expectations, while allowing for the chance to recognize those worth your time. There is safety in numbers and it allows you to spend time with people without the pressures of an official date. Though many students meet their mate in college, many do not. Keep your goal in mind—mate or degree!

THE DANGEROUS 5

There is little chance that you will survive the hopefully less than four-years without exposure to the **DANGEROUS 5:**

1. **Alcohol**
2. **Drugs**
3. **Love**
4. **Peer pressure**
5. **Sex**

When struggling over difficult decisions, consider this advice from my mom "——give it the *'newspaper test'*. Imagine that you are sitting on your porch, with family and friends and the newspaper is delivered and you are featured on the front page. As you reflect on the article and your life, will you regret doing or not doing it? Pick the decision you can live with, and have no regrets in your choice."

Too often, students do not realize the negative effects of the Dangerous 5 until it's too late. Your response to these challenges will carry a lot of weight. It can determine not only whether you will finish in less than four-years, but also whether you will finish at all. I can remember when "Miss America" lost her crown because of a picture that had been taken of her during her late teen years. It is your call! Use common sense as you keep your values and goals clearly in mind.

To respond to situations you have the - **APA** (Aggressive, Passive, Assertive) **options**. An aggressive response to a Dangerous 5 option places your true feelings upfront, either directly or indirectly, but it would probably anger the individual who made the offer. A *passive* response is a nice "no thank you." It will probably allow you to avoid immediate hassle, but does not express your true feelings and as a result you may receive the same offer again. An *assertive* response requires that you state your feelings directly. It says that you are definitely not interested and that's final. Your response would be honest, direct, and probably respected.

Developing effective coping strategies might not be easy, but it is definitely necessary. Your personal values and an understanding of the possible consequences should be your guide. The indiscretion of youth can make a huge impact on your future. Whether you realize it or not, decisions made during college can affect your entire life. How you will cope with social issues and friendships are in some cases the most difficult decisions you must make.

And then there is *love* , young girls new to the campus are a challenge for upper classmen. Remember, they all have girl friends, but as a new kid on the block they are anxious to help you get acclimated to college life. Watch IT!! Try really hard not to fall in love the first year on the college campus, have lots of friends, meet as many new people as possible, and keep your goals in view.

Responses like the following are often used in an attempt to influence another's moral decisions:

You are an adult now!
Are you chicken?
If you love me you would!

It may be very difficult resisting this type of pressure. Just remember your **APA** response options. There is no doubt that college provides the chance for you to try new things; a host of opportunities will be available. There are organizations to join, intramural sports to play, work with the student newspaper, participation in a drama, running for student government, work on a political campaign, and many other extra-curricular activities.

As you are probably already aware, drugs are one of the most destructive options you will face. Possession, use, transmitting or being under the influence

89

of any narcotic drug, hallucinogenic drug, barbiturate, marijuana, any controlled substance or any alcoholic beverage can mean disaster for a student. Many still make the mistake. Despite the fact that there is wide availability and use of these items on some campuses it is still illegal and will probably result in the end of your education. It is well known that pranks in college can result in an unknowing intake of drugs. Always be aware of this possibility when with a group where food and drinks are consumed. **Be in control of your personal well being at all times**. Think before trying any addictive substances. Watch those who take addictive substances and see how stupid they act! Let your guide be – *"would I want to see this on the front page of the newspaper?"*

However, before participating in any of the **Dangerous 5** activities you must remember your primary goal – to finish in less than four-years. If your choices do not help bring you closer to this goal, they will probably prevent you from achieving it.

SUMMARY

Perhaps you started this book saying *of course you can do it in less time if you attend a community college or go to summer school each year.* Having spent a significant part of my professional life as a community college administrator, I found that a great many students spend two years at the community college and have to spend an additional three years completing the requirements at the university for the four-year degree.

However, if one decides to attend summer school each year it will decrease the amount of time required for the degree. The goal here is to share with you a plan for starting and finishing at the same college where you have established yourself as a serious student. As long as you are committed to a goal, you can accomplish what you set out to do. Once committed, it's full steam ahead. This is not to say that there will not be bumps along the road. Well-defined goals can give you the map to overcome the hurdles that you will face. It has long been said that anything worth having requires more than you had anticipated. And the results are often far more rewarding than you had imagined. To be successful in the game of college, you must have your goals clearly in focus, recognize your abilities, and be committed to achieving your goals.

10 ESSENTIALS FOR A COLLEGE DEGREE IN 3

1. START PLANNING EARLY
Your career plan should be well in hand before the end of 12th grade.

2. KNOW THE HIGH SCHOOL OPTIONS
AP classes and Dual Enrollment can decrease the time required for the college degree.

3. RESEARCH FINANCIAL RESOURCES
Start in 9th grade developing a list of financial sources to support your college education.

4. DEVELOP TIME MANAGEMENT SKILLS & A DISCIPLINED STUDY PLAN
Time is a constant. The productive people take advantage of each moment.

5. MAKE A SMART COLLEGE CHOICE
There are thousands of colleges, check carefully for the best choice for you.

6. HAVE A COLLEGE MAJOR CLEARLY IN MIND
Deciding a major before enrolling in college can decrease the time in college.

7. VISUALIZE YOUR GOALS
Recognize the value of imagery – picture yourself finishing college in 3 years.

8. RECOGNIZE THE IMPORTANCE OF THE COLLEGE CATALOGUE
The college catalogue is key to developing a realistic schedule for completing college in a timely manner.

9. KNOW CAMPUS RESOURCES
The campus provides valuable academic, financial and personal resources locate and use these.

10. KNOW YOUR INSTRUCTORS
Get to know the people who are responsible for your academic program.

APPENDIX

From the word lists, identify the words and word parts that are already a part of your vocabulary. Then develop a technique for adding a specific number of new words to your vocabulary each week. Students who lack a familiarity with the terminology used in classes tend to have trouble with college assignments.

GENERAL VOCABULARY WORDS

Words that should be a part of your vocabulary.

acquiesce	chagrin	elusive	genealogy	ironic	niche	serendipity
adamant	chancery	eminent	geocentric	itinerant	nostalgia	stipend
aficionado	coercion	empathy	gigantic	jaunt	obsolete	stoic
alcove	contrite	emulate	gregarious	jostle	paltry	subvert
alliteration	cosign	entourage	grouse	juncture	partisan	symmetrical
aplomb	credulity	equilibrium	gullible	juxtapose	perception	squalor
aroma	curricular	esoteric	heresy	kilogram	plateau	terse
astute	delineate	exemplary	hypothetical	levity	plethora	tome
atrophy	derogatory	fastidious	impede	liaison	prognosis	travesty
aversion	detriment	felicitous	implicit	liaison	pungent	unison
badger	disdain	fervor	incite	lurid	quantum	vacuity
beguile	disperse	fidelity	indolent	malice	quench	vertigo
bigotry	divulge	flagrant	inference	morose	recluse	wane
boisterous	dogmatic	florid	integrity	mundane	resplendent	xenophobia
brevity	eclectic	gauche	invincible	naïve	scarcity	zenith

SUBJECT VOCABULARY WORDS

Examples of words used while studying college subjects.

Psychology		History		Ecology	
affiliation	divergent	abdicate	evacuation	aesthetics	exponential
altruism	empathy	abstract	ideologies	archaeology	habitat
catharsis	fallacy	alliance	kinship	celibacy	implementation
cognition	fraternal	aristocracy	parliamentary	compression	inequities
concurrent	gestalt	bureaucracy	provisional	condensation	innovation
contingency	humanistic	concessions	reconciliation	consequences	opportunistic
correlation	lethargy	conservatism	solidarity	decompose	simulation
covert	somatic	consolidation	unification	demographic	suppression
criterion		culmination		diversity	

COMMON PREFIXES

ad ....to	hydro ....water	pre ....before
amb ....both	hyper ....overly	pro ....forward
anti ....against	inter ....between	pseudo ....false (ly)
bi ....two	intra ....within	re ....again
circum ....around	macro ....large	retro ....back
co ....together	mal ....bad(ly)	semi ....partly
de ....remove	mono ....one; single	sub ....under
dis ....opposite of	non ....not	sym ....together
ex ....former	omni ....all	syn ....with
extra ....beyond	poly ....many	thermo ....heat
homo ....same	post......................after	trans ....across

COMMON SUFFIXES

-able .... capable	-oid ....shape or form
-algia ....pain	-phobia ....fear
-arium ....place of	-ment ....action
-ation ....process	-meter ....to measure
-dom ....quality; state	-oid ....shape
-ify ....to make	-phile ....loving
-ism ....the act, theory of	-ity ....quality
-ology ....study of	-ular ....relating to

93

LATIN AND GREEK ROOTS

-anthropo- ....human	neg- ....no
-arch-/archi- ....ancient times	phon- ....sound
-audi- ....hearing, sound	phys- ....body
-bene- ....good	port- ....carry
-bio- ....life	pseudo- ....false
-chrono- ....time	scrib- ....to write
-derm- ....skin	-sect ....cut
-dict- ....to say	sol- ....alone
gen- ....kind, type; birth	-struct ....build
-geo- ....earth	-tract ....to pull, drag
-log ....study	vert- ....to turn
macro- ....large	vid- ....see

SCHOLARSHIPS LISTING

Guide to Financial Aid	http://www.collegescholarships.org
	http://www.collegescholarships.com/
	http://www.QuestBridge.org
	http://www.studentscholarshipsearch.com/
	http://www.scholarshipBootcamp.com/
	http://www.salliemae.com
	http://www.FastWeb.com
	http://www.uncf.org
	http://www.scholarship.us.com
	http://www.nationalmerit.org
Student Inventors	http://www.invent.org/collegiate/
Coca-Cola	http://www.coca-colascholars.org/
Microsoft	http://www.microsoft.com/collegescholarships/
William R. Hearst	http://www.apsanet.org/opps
Guaranteed Scholarships	http://www.guaranteed-scholarships.com/
Gates Millennium	http://www.gmsp.org
Burger King	http://www.bkscholars.scholarshipamerica.org
	http://www.bk.com/scholars
Washington Post	http://www.washingtonpost.com
Westinghouse	http://www.siemens-foundation.org/
Rhodes Scholarship	http://www.rhodesscholar.org/info.html
Roothbert Scholarship	http://www.roothbertfund.org/school
Ronald McDonald	http://www.rmhc.org

LIST OF CHARTS

95

INDEX

96

REFERENCES

Artze, Isis and Bravo, Jorge. (2001). Guide to the top 25 Colleges for Hispanics. General Motors Presentation. Detroit, MI.

Bowman, J. W. (1999). America's Black and Tribal Colleges. Sandcastle. S.Pasadena, CA.

Bennett, J. M. (1994). Four Powers of Communication Skills for Effective Learning. McGraw-Hill, New York, NY.

Chickering, A.W. and Schlossberg, N.K. (1995). Getting the Most Out of College. Allyn and Bacon, NY.

Chickering, A.W. and Reisser, Linda (1993). Education and Identity. Jossey Bass. San Francisco, CA.

Davis, M. and McKay, M. (2000). Relaxation and Stress Reduction. New Harbinger Publication, Inc. Oakland, CA.

Donald, Robert et. al. (1983). Writing Clear Essays. Prentice Hall, Inc. Newark, NJ.

Kaplan, Ben (2007) How To Go To College Almost For Free. Harper Resource. An Imprint of HarperCollins Publication. Atlanta, GA.

Lazarus, R.S. and Folkman, S. (1984). Stress, Appraisal, and Coping. Springer Press. New York, NY.

Newport, Cal (2007). How to Become a Straight-A Student. Doubleday Broadway Publishing Group. A division of Random House, Inc., New York, NY.

Princeton Review (2008). 11 Practice Tests for the SAT and PSAT. Random House. New York, NY

Rimal, R.N. and Orton, P.Z. (1996). 30 Days to the SAT. Simon & Schuster. New York, NY.

Schrefer, Eliot, (2008). Hack the SAT. Gotham Books. New York, NY.

Shepherd, J. F. (1987). Study Skills Handbook. Houghton Mifflin Co. New York, NY.

Printed in the United States
146376LV00003B/12/P

9 780966 356212